Favourite Food
from Ambrose Heath

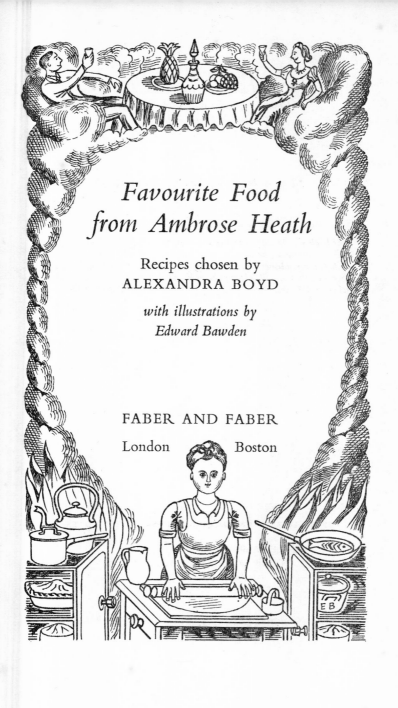

Favourite Food from Ambrose Heath

Recipes chosen by
ALEXANDRA BOYD

with illustrations by
Edward Bawden

FABER AND FABER

London   Boston

First published in 1979
by Faber and Faber Limited
3 Queen Square London WC1N 3AU
Printed in Great Britain by
Latimer Trend & Company Ltd Plymouth
All rights reserved

BRITISH LIBRARY CATALOGUING IN PUBLICATION DATA

Heath, Ambrose
  Favourite Food from Ambrose Heath
  1. Cookery
  I. Title   II. Boyd, Alexandra
  641.5   TX717

  ISBN 0–571–11427–X
  ISBN 0–571–11428–8 Pbk

Contents

Introduction

As a child I loved to browse amongst my mother's well-used cookery books, and it was here that I discovered the delights of Ambrose Heath. *Good Sweets and Ices* was my firm favourite. What child could help but be inspired by Toffee Pudding, Marmalade Cream or indeed L'Ami des Enfants?

As I grew up and my interest in cookery matured I enjoyed his other books, when I could find them. *Good Soups*, *Good Vegetables*, *Good Food* and *Good Food Again*, the list goes on. Ambrose Heath was a prolific writer; he wrote over seventy books and his ingenuity was boundless.

I collect cookery books like other people collect stamps, and what joy to find an Ambrose Heath lurking on a dusty shelf in some little back street second-hand bookshop. These slim volumes with their lovely thick paper and charming illustrations by Edward Bawden delighted me, and the recipes never failed to rouse my sometimes jaded enthusiasm for cooking my own family meals.

To select these recipes I have re-read all Ambrose Heath's books and I chose the dishes that I would cook for my own family and friends. Few people of my generation will have heard of Ambrose Heath, or if they have they associate him somewhat vaguely with wartime cookery, but I feel that this food is today's food, good home cooking but using the wonderful variety of herbs, spices and vegetables that are so widely available in our local shops these days. Many of the meat recipes I have chosen use cheaper cuts of meat such as in Lamb and Apricot Stew, or pulse vegetables as in

Mutton and Beans. I believe there is a great revival of interest in the pulses, not only as a high source of protein but for their delicious flavour and texture. Maybe there will be another revival for rabbit or dumplings, foods which have been out of fashion recently. There are more extravagant dishes in this book too—after all, we all like to be lavish sometimes.

Ambrose Heath did not often list ingredients, quantities or oven temperatures so I have added these and any other notes which I feel will be helpful, but I hope they will not detract from the original charm of the recipes. The quantities I have suggested are for four people, unless otherwise stated.

I must stress that this is a personal choice and I hope that I have not offended too many of Ambrose Heath's fans by leaving out their particular favourite, and above all I hope that anyone who is discovering him for the first time will enjoy cooking and eating these meals as much as he so obviously did himself.

Oven Temperatures

°C	°F	Gas mark	
110	225	¼	very cool
120	250	½	very cool
140	275	1	cool
150	300	2	slow
170	325	3	moderately slow
180	350	4	moderate
190	375	5	moderately hot
200	400	6	hot
220	425	7	very hot
230	450	8	very hot

Weights and Measures

It was felt that changing Ambrose Heath's measurements into metric would spoil their charm, so therefore a metric conversion table is included here. The conversions are not exact equivalents but are intended to produce the same proportions of ingredients (exact equivalents: 1 oz = 28·35 g; 1 pt = ·568 l).

ounces	grams	pints	litres
1	25		
1½	35		
2	50		
3	75	½	¼
4	100	1	½
5	150	2	1
6	175	3¾	2
7	200		
8	225		
12	350		
16	450		

The Miniature Herb Garden
from Ambrose Heath's *Simple Salads*

For those without gardens, a supply of pots or a window-box or two are quite sufficient to provide enough herbs for general use in a small household. These are the herbs I should counsel growing.

PARSLEY   Sow if you like, but perhaps the transplantation of a few young plants is more satisfactory, as they start growing right away. By the way, I have never found the superstition about transplanting parsley being unlucky borne out by fact. Keep the plants well picked to encourage growth, but not picked too hard, and pick out any flowering heads that may appear. [This applies to other herbs as well.]

THYME   Usually better to keep this in a pot of its own, as it prefers a slightly different soil to other herbs. In the absence of lemons, see if you can get a plant of lemon thyme as well as common thyme.

CHERVIL   This grows like parsley.

MINT   Once this is established, you will have no difficulty with it at all, so long as you keep it moist.

MARJORAM   Like thyme. Get pot marjoram as this is a perennial.

SAGE   Irrepressible.

CHIVES   Three or four clumps of these will provide you with enough choppings for the summer. By putting a piece of glass over their pot or box in the late winter, you will be able to hasten the appearance of the little spiky leaves.

CORN SALAD   If you have room, grow some of this as a winter salad. It grows easily, and does not take up too much room. Sow in August for a winter supply.

DANDELION In the miniature herb garden room may be occasionally found for a dandelion root transplanted into a pot. When this has settled down, and begins to grow again, put a tile or stone over the top of the pot and let the dandelion leaves blanch. You will find that they provide a salad not unlike our old friend chicory or endive. A succession of plants can be kept growing in the pot or pots, and so always be ready to provide a green salad at a moment's notice.

SORREL If you like the pleasantly astringent flavour of a little sorrel in a salad, you should certainly make room for a plant or two in a pot or box. The broad-leaved sorrel is the best to get, and there is no reason why, with a minimum of care, you should not be able to gather a few leaves all the year round.

[TARRAGON Where tarragon is used in these recipes it is recommended that French tarragon is used rather than Russian tarragon which can have rather a bitter flavour.]

Soups

*Buttermilk Soup · Fish Soup · Mussel Soup · Garbure · Kidney
Soup · Philadelphia Pepper Pot · Beetroot Soup · Cabbage Soup ·
Chantilly Soup · Chestnut Soup · Melon Soup · Potage aux
Herbes · Potage Basque · Potato Soup · Soupe aux Poireaux
(Leek Soup) · Spinach Soup · Spring Vegetable Soup · Tomato
Soup · Turnip Soup · Vegetable Chowder · Cold Sorrel Soup ·
Cheese and Garlic Soup · Garnishes for Soups: Cheese Sticks,
Bread Croûtons, Potato Croûtons, Meat Balls, Suet Dumplings*

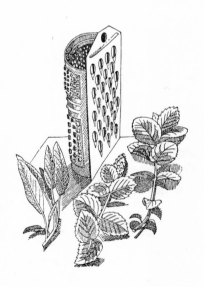

BUTTERMILK SOUP

½ lb picked, chopped shrimps or prawns
½ peeled medium-sized cucumber
3 teaspoons made mustard
3 teaspoons minced fresh dill
2 pt buttermilk
1 teaspoon salt
1 teaspoon sugar

Mix together half a pound of picked and chopped shrimps or prawns, half a peeled medium-sized cucumber cut in fine dice, three teaspoonfuls each of made mustard and minced fresh dill, and a teaspoonful each of salt and sugar. Stir in gradually a quart of buttermilk, and chill thoroughly before serving.

FISH SOUP

2 oz butter
2 pieces of whiting, plaice or lemon sole
Bunch chervil [or parsley]
1 quart bottle cider
Salt and pepper

An uncommon soup, very simple to make. Warm the butter in a saucepan, add salt and pepper and cook some pieces of fish gently in it for about five minutes. Pour in the cider, add the chervil [or parsley] and simmer gently for about twenty minutes, or until the fish is done. Serve as it is, less the chervil but with the pieces of fish.

MUSSEL SOUP

[Mussels should always be bought fresh with their shells tightly closed. If you come across one with its shell open, give it a sharp

tap with the back of a knife. If it is alive the shell will close immediately; if it stays open throw it away as the mussel is dead.

To clean mussels, scrape off any filament or beard that may be
attached to the shell and wash them several times in clean cold
water until there is no grit or sand.]

    1 quart mussels
    1 pt water
    1 onion
    A sprig of parsley
    1 clove
    1 bayleaf
    A little thyme
    Salt and pepper
    1 glass dry white wine
    A little cream to finish
    Chopped parsley

Mussel soup is so cheap that we shall be able to afford the glass of
wine we must use in it. Clean the mussels well, and cook them for
a quarter of an hour or so in a pint of water to which you have
added an onion, chopped, a good sprig of parsley, a clove, a bayleaf, a little thyme, salt, pepper and a glass of dry white wine.
When they open their shells they are cooked, discard any that do
not open, take them out of their shells and keep them warm.
Reduce the soup a little, strain it, and add a little cream, chopped
parsley and the mussels.

GARBURE

[The haricot beans should be washed and soaked overnight in cold
water for this recipe; the more thorough the soaking the less time
they will take to cook. Make sure they are well covered by the
water as they will absorb quite a lot of it during the soaking.]

4 oz soaked haricot beans
1 medium cabbage
2 carrots
1 piece of pickled pork, about 1 lb
Bouquet of parsley, thyme, bayleaf
Salt and pepper

Cook the well-soaked haricot beans in salted water, and put in a medium-sized chopped cabbage and two carrots cut in small pieces. Cook on a quick fire until the beans are cooked and about an hour before you want it, put in a piece of pickled pork, some salt, pepper and the bouquet. More boiling water can be added to ensure the soup being of the right consistence. The meat and the bouquet must of course be removed before serving.

KIDNEY SOUP

2 calf's kidneys
1 oz butter
2 chopped shallots
Good pinch of mixed sweet herbs
2 tablespoons flour
4 pt hot stock
2 egg yolks mixed with a little warm milk
Fried bread croûtons

Slice two calf's kidneys and cook them until slightly browned in the butter, with two chopped shallots and the mixed sweet herbs. Then sprinkle with two tablespoonfuls of flour, and let that brown too. Add the hot stock, and simmer for half an hour. Season to taste, and bind before serving with two egg yolks mixed with a little warm milk. Hand fried bread croûtons.

PHILADELPHIA PEPPER POT

[Tripe has been rather out of favour in the last few years but I have noticed a revival of interest in it now that meat and fish are so expensive. It is an acquired taste but one well worth acquiring.]

1 sliced onion
3–4 tablespoons chopped celery
3–4 tablespoons chopped green peppers
1½ breakfastcups potato cut up in cubes
3 tablespoons butter
3½ tablespoons flour
½ lb honeycomb tripe cut in cubes
2 pt chicken stock
Salt and pepper
½ cup cream
Extra pieces of butter for finishing

Have ready a sliced onion, three or four tablespoonfuls of chopped celery and green peppers, a breakfastcupful and a half of potato cubes, and fry these together for a quarter of an hour in three tablespoonfuls of butter. Then add three and a half tablespoonfuls of flour, and mix all well together. Now put in half a pound of honeycomb tripe cut in cubes, and two pints of chicken stock, season with salt and pepper. Cover and simmer for an hour, and just before serving add half a cupful of fresh cream and finish with a tablespoonful of butter in small pieces.

BEETROOT SOUP

3 beetroots
1 head of celery
1 pt water mixed with 1 pt milk
1 tablespoon of cream
A little butter to finish

If we cannot afford the time or the expense of preparing an elaborate Russian *bortsch*, we can try a more modest beetroot soup. Boil three beetroots in water for three hours, then peel them and chop them up with a head of celery. Have a pint of water and the same measure of milk in a saucepan, and cook the beetroot and celery in this till they are soft enough to pass through a sieve. [You can use a blender if you have one.] Having done this to them, add a spoonful of cream and a little butter and serve.

CABBAGE SOUP

[Pickled pork is sometimes known as 'poor man's bacon'. It is eaten cold, cut in very thin slices; it is rather fat but sweet. I think I should find it more appetizing as a luncheon dish than the breakfast that Ambrose Heath suggests.]

> 1 lb pickled pork
> Bouquet of parsley, thyme and bayleaf
> 1 carrot, chopped
> 1 small turnip, chopped
> 1 white cabbage, finely shredded
> Little chopped parsley
> 1 clove of garlic
> Salt and pepper

Cabbage makes a good winter soup, which has the merit of providing a second course for breakfast as well, for those who like cold pickled pork. Put a pound of pickled pork in a saucepan of cold water with a bouquet of parsley, thyme and bayleaf. Cook this for an hour, and then take out the pork and the bouquet. Have ready a carrot and a small turnip cut in small pieces, and a good white cabbage finely shredded. Add these to the liquor from the pork with salt and pepper, and cook for another two hours. About half an hour before the soup is wanted, throw in some chopped parsley, a chopped clove of garlic (if you like it) and a little of the pork also cut up fine.

CHANTILLY SOUP

2 pt chicken stock
1 pt shelled peas
A handful of prepared spinach, about 4 oz
Sprig of parsley
2–3 mint leaves
1 small chopped onion
1 tablespoon cream
Salt and pepper

A very pleasant soup for an unexpectedly cool summer evening. In two pints of stock boil a pint of shelled peas (save a few for the garnish), a small handful of prepared spinach, a sprig of parsley, two or three mint leaves and a small chopped onion. When the peas are tender, rub the whole thing through a sieve [or use a blender if you have one], and when serving bind with a tablespoonful or so of cream, season to taste and add a few whole cooked peas as a garnish.

CHESTNUT SOUP

¾ lb chestnuts, cooked and peeled [see below]
1½ pt white stock [or chicken stock]
1 small onion, chopped
1 stick of celery, sliced
Sprig of parsley
¾ pt milk
2 tablespoons cream
Salt and pepper

Cook and peel three-quarters of a pound of chestnuts and pass them through a sieve. Put this purée into a saucepan and add to it a pint and a half of white stock, a small onion chopped, a stick of celery sliced, a sprig of parsley and a seasoning of salt and pepper.

Simmer for an hour and a half, add three-quarters of a pint of milk, sieve, reheat and mix in a couple of tablespoonfuls of cream just before serving.

[The simplest way to cook and peel chestnuts is to peel the nuts first by putting them in cold water and bringing them quickly to the boil. Take the chestnuts out one at a time and the peel will come off easily. Keep the other chestnuts hot but not boiling. If the water gets too cold bring it back to the boil. These peeled chestnuts can then be simmered until they are soft and ready to be sieved or put through a blender.]

MELON SOUP

1 medium-sized melon, preferably a cantaloup
1 oz butter
Little chopped chervil
1½ pt of milk
1 egg yolk
2–3 tablespoons of cream
Salt and pepper

Cut up in smallish pieces the flesh of a medium-sized not too ripe melon, preferably a cantaloup. Cook these for a few minutes in the butter, add a little chopped chervil, season with salt and pepper and moisten with a pint and a half of boiling milk. Bring gently to the boil, and simmer slowly for half an hour. Then pass it through a fine sieve [or blender], and bind with the egg yolk and cream mixed together. It can be garnished with small chervil leaves, little cubes of melon fried in butter and croûtons of fried bread.

[To mix in the egg yolk and cream, first work them together in a bowl, then add three or four tablespoonfuls of the soup to the yolk and when it is well mixed return it to the saucepan off the heat. Mix it well together, then heat the soup slowly stirring it continuously, but do not allow it to boil as it will curdle.]

POTAGE AUX HERBES

[This is a lovely soup for a summer evening.]

A handful of sorrel leaves [see page 16 for notes on a
   miniature herb garden]
½ lettuce
½ bunch watercress (no stalks)
A handful of chervil [or parsley]
2 pt hot water
3 medium potatoes, quartered
Salt
1 oz butter

Cut a handful of sorrel leaves and the lettuce in fine strips, and
chop up rather coarsely the leaves of the watercress and chervil.
Let them 'melt' for half an hour in half the butter then moisten
with the hot water. Add three medium-sized potatoes peeled and
cut in quarters, and salt to your taste. Cover and boil gently for
half an hour. Rub through a fine sieve [or use a blender], boil up
for a minute, and finish off the fire with the rest of the butter.

POTAGE BASQUE

8 oz French beans, strung and cut in lozenges
1½ pt boiling water
2 peeled potatoes, chopped
1 clove of garlic
A few thin slices of bread
Grated cheese
A few stoned olives
Salt and pepper

String the French beans and cut them into lozenges, put them on
the fire with the boiling water, and add the chopped potatoes and

a clove of garlic. Season with salt and pepper, put on the lid and cook for an hour. When the soup is cooked, mash the potatoes in it with a fork. Cut some thin slices of bread and put them in the bottom of the tureen, sprinkle them with grated cheese, and pour a little of the soup over them. Leave them for a minute or two, and then pour in the rest of the soup, adding some stoned olives.

POTATO SOUP

> 1 onion, chopped
> 1 tablespoon lard
> 4–5 potatoes, peeled and cut in cubes
> 2 pt water or stock
> Paprika pepper
> Salt
> 3 tablespoons sour cream
> Sprig parsley

A Hungarian version. Chop up an onion and stew it without browning in a tablespoonful of lard. Add some paprika pepper and four or five potatoes pared and cut in small cubes. Add a sprig of parsley, and continue to stew it for a while. Then pour in the stock or water, season with salt, and simmer until the potatoes are soft. Add three tablespoonfuls of sour cream, and serve.

SOUPE AUX POIREAUX (LEEK SOUP)

> A handful of sorrel
> Two handfuls of chervil [or parsley]
> 6 medium-sized leeks
> 2 lettuces
> 1 oz butter
> 4 pt water
> 6 medium-sized potatoes, peeled and quartered
> Salt, pepper, pinch of basil

This really excellent and very simple soup comes from Flanders. Chop up a handful of sorrel, two of chervil, half a dozen medium-sized leeks and a couple of lettuces, and cook them in the salted water with a little butter and a seasoning of salt, pepper and a pinch of basil. Add also half a dozen medium-sized potatoes, peeled and cut in quarters. Let all this cook very slowly for four or five hours, then mash up the potatoes as they are in the soup, quite roughly, and serve as it is.

SPINACH SOUP

1 lb spinach
1 oz butter
2½ pt hot water
1 breakfastcup milk
cream or egg yolk for binding

This is better than the cream of spinach soup usually recommended. Cook the prepared spinach (that is, well washed and the ribs removed) on a slow fire with the butter until the spinach 'melts'. Then chop it finely, add the hot water, simmer for half an hour and then add the breakfastcupful of milk. Boil again until it is reduced by about a third, season well and bind with cream or egg yolk before serving.

SPRING VEGETABLE SOUP

2 young carrots
2 turnips
White part of 2 leeks
Heart of a young cabbage
1 oz butter
Lettuce heart
2 oz fresh peas
Chervil [or parsley]

2½ pt chicken stock
1 beaten egg yolk

Scrape some young carrots and turnips and cut them in thin slices,
also the white part of two leeks treated in the same way, and the
heart of a young cabbage cut in four. Cook these slowly in the
butter in a covered saucepan till they are tender. Then add a
quartered lettuce heart, the peas and a little chervil chopped up,
and finally the stock. Reduce the soup by a third on a slow fire (it
will take a good time), and just before you are ready for it—
practically on its way from the saucepan to the tureen—mix well
in with it the beaten yolk of an egg.

TOMATO SOUP

2 leeks, the white part only
1 tablespoon olive oil
1 tablespoonful of flour
1 cupful stock
5–6 peeled and quartered tomatoes
1 stick celery
Bouquet parsley, thyme and bayleaf
1 clove garlic, optional
2 pt water
Croûtons of bread or a handful of rice and a few cubes of
    bacon

As this soup comes from Provence, the use of olive oil is essential
if the authentic flavour is to be captured. But it might be made
with butter. Fry lightly the white part of two leeks in a little oil,
sprinkle with the flour and add a cupful of stock. When this is
boiling, add five or six quartered tomatoes, a stick of celery, salt,
pepper and the bouquet, with, if you like it, a bruised clove of
garlic. When this boils anew, pour in the water, cover and simmer
for half an hour. Take out the bouquet with the garlic, and serve

with croûtons of bread, fried in oil. Or instead of the croûtons, you can add twenty minutes before serving, a handful of rice and a few little cubes of lean bacon fried beforehand in oil.

TURNIP SOUP

2 oz butter
6 young turnips
Salt
Pinch sugar
2½ pt water, boiling
Small cubes of fried bread
Egg yolk and cream mixed

Turnips have an entirely masculine flavour, peppery and very definite, delicious not merely as a vegetable course, their harshness softened with butter, but as a soup, simple enough, which will shame most others in April when they are at their best. Cook in butter [one and a half ounces], but not long enough to brown them, six young turnips quartered. Add plenty of salt, the rest of the butter and a pinch of sugar. Fill up with the boiling water and simmer for four hours. When it is done, pass the turnips through a fine sieve [or blend them], and water down with the liquid they have cooked in till the soup has the right consistency. Tiny croûtons of fried bread with this please, and you can enrich it with an egg yolk beaten with a little cream. [Do not boil the soup after the egg yolk has been added (see page 24).]

VEGETABLE CHOWDER

[This is a substantial soup, very warming and should be quite thick with the vegetables. Fresh okra, or ladies' fingers as it is often called, is sold in Indian and West Indian food shops and also in some supermarkets and can be used instead of the canned variety.]

3 rashers of thickish bacon
1 cup sliced tinned okra
2 cups tomatoes, peeled and chopped
½ cup shelled peas
2 sliced onions
1 stick celery, chopped
2 green peppers, chopped
3 potatoes in small cubes
4 pt water

Cut three thickish rashers of bacon into cubes, and fry them until they are crisp and brown. To these add a cupful of sliced tinned okra, two cupfuls of tomato, half a cupful of shelled peas, a couple of thinly sliced onions, a finely chopped stick of celery, a couple of green peppers chopped up, three potatoes in small cubes and the water. Cook the whole thing slowly until the vegetables are soft [about an hour], then season to taste and serve at once.

COLD SORREL SOUP

1 lb washed sorrel
1 pt cream [single]

Take the stalks and ribs from some sorrel, and set aside a pound of it. Wash it well and mash and pound it as finely as possible. Mix it with one pint of cream, salt it, and serve it very cold.

CHEESE AND GARLIC SOUP

2 pt water
2 oz garlic
A few leaves of sage
2 cloves
¼ oz salt
Pepper

A few slices of bread
Grated cheese

This highly anti-social soup is included out of deference to mis-
anthropes and garlic-lovers. It will not be generally approved, but
some will welcome a recipe for it. Put two pints of water into a
saucepan with two ounces of garlic clove, peeled, a few leaves of
sage, a couple of cloves and a quarter of an ounce of salt and a little
pepper. Simmer for twenty minutes. Put into the soup tureen a
few slices of bread which have been sprinkled well with grated
cheese and then put into the oven until the cheese has melted, and
strain the soup over them, pressing the cloves of garlic gently
against the sieve but not rubbing them through. Leave for a
minute until the bread has absorbed the liquid, and serve very hot.

GARNISHES FOR SOUPS

CHEESE STICKS

Cut some slices of bread into little sticks, spread them thinly with
butter, sprinkle them with grated cheese seasoned with salt and
cayenne pepper, and bake them until lightly browned.

BREAD CROÛTONS (FRIED)

Croûtons of bread should be all the same size and cut from stale
bread. The best frying medium is clarified butter. Put the butter
in a frying-pan on a very moderate fire, and when it begins to get
hot, put in the croûtons. When they are lightly browned, toss
them about so that they are brown all over; if they are too large
to toss, turn them over with a fork. Never fry them in deep fat, as
some cookery books misguidedly advise. Olive oil or lard may
sometimes be used, if directed in the recipe of the soup. Keep the

croûtons hot in the pan (having poured off the fat), so that they do not soften before being served with the soup.

[To clarify butter melt it in a pan and cook it gently, skimming the impurities off the top as they rise. Strain the butter through a sieve lined with muslin and leave it in a basin to settle, then pour it carefully into a clean basin, leaving the sediment behind.]

POTATO CROÛTONS

These are often used instead of bread croûtons, and are very attractive. Cut the potatoes into tiny dice of about an eighth of an inch sides, throw them as they are done into cold water, then drain them and dry them in a cloth. A quarter of an hour before you want them, heat the clarified butter in a frying-pan, put the dice into it, salt them very lightly, and let them cook on the side of the stove or on a very slight heat, tossing them from time to time. They should get gradually golden, and when done are quite crisp outside while the inside is still soft.

MEAT BALLS

[I find soup with meat balls makes a good simple luncheon dish.] Mince a quarter of a pound of raw beef very finely, and mix it with two ounces of fine breadcrumbs, a teaspoon of grated onion, twice that amount of chopped parsley, the grated rind of half a lemon, and a seasoning of salt, pepper and nutmeg. Bind with a beaten egg, roll into marbles and cook for twenty minutes in the soup.

SUET DUMPLINGS

(See page 50.)

Small Meals and Savouries

For other vegetable dishes that would be suitable to serve at luncheon see the Vegetable chapter

Chicken Livers on Toast · Kidney in Potato · Sausage in Potato · Sausages and Apples · Ham Ramekins · Little Ham Loaves · Home-made Pâté de Foie Gras · Country Pâté · Terrine of Hare · Anchoiade · Potted Shrimps on Toast · Cauliflower with Shrimps · Smoked Haddock Puffs · Potted Sprats · Potatoes Florentine · Stuffed Baby Pumpkins · Leek Pancake · Stuffed Tomatoes · Tomatoes with Scrambled Eggs · Eggs à la Tripe · Sorrel Omelette · Omelette Grand'mère · Omelette Chartres · Spinach Soufflé · Macaroni · Croûte Fromagée · Cheese Wafers · Camembert in Aspic · Fried Camembert

CHICKEN LIVERS ON TOAST

Flour
8 oz chicken livers
Salt, pepper, paprika
1 oz butter for frying
3 tablespoons stock
½ glass sherry
Buttered toast
Small grilled mushrooms if liked

Roll the livers lightly in flour seasoned with salt, pepper and paprika. Melt some butter, not too much, in a frying-pan and cook the livers in it till they are nicely browned. Add a few tablespoonfuls of stock and half a glass of sherry. Cook together slowly for about a quarter of an hour, and serve the livers on pieces of buttered toast. There would be no harm in surmounting each toast with small grilled mushrooms.

KIDNEY IN POTATO

1 sheep's kidney per person
1 large potato per person

A good dish—no, a good meal! Take a very large potato, cut off a good slice of the top and scoop out a hole large enough to enclose a sheep's kidney on which you have left a little of the fat. Put the kidney into the potato, season it with salt and pepper, put the top on again, and tie it firmly. Now bake the potato very slowly in the oven [Mark 3 or 325°F (170°C)], and when the potato is done, the kidney will be found to be gloriously ready, too.

SAUSAGE IN POTATO

1 large potato per person
About ½ lb sausage meat for 4

Bacon fat if available
[Cut clove of garlic, optional]

Have ready some peeled potatoes all the same size, and make a hole
in each with an apple corer, but don't push it quite all the way
through. Push in enough sausage meat to fill the hole, and bake
the potatoes in a hot oven [Mark 5 or 375°F (190°C)] until they
are done, basting them every ten minutes with a little sausage
dripping or bacon fat. [I have found myself that this dish is con-
siderably improved if the hole in the potato is introduced for a
moment to a cut clove of garlic before the sausage is inserted.]

SAUSAGES AND APPLES

1 lb sausages
2 cooking apples, cored not peeled
A little milk
Flour for dipping
Fried bread, optional

Prick and fry the sausages in the usual way. Take them out and
keep them hot. Core a couple of cooking apples, but do not skin
them, and cut them into thickish slices. Dip them in a little milk
and then in flour, and fry them in the sausage fat. Dish them with
the sausages and a few triangles of fried bread or toast. Bananas
can be used in the same way.

HAM RAMEKINS

2½ oz finely chopped lean ham
2 tablespoons milk
¼ teaspoon mixed herbs
½ teaspoon made mustard
1 lightly beaten egg yolk
1 stiffly beaten egg white
Salt and pepper

To a lightly beaten egg yolk, add two and a half ounces of finely chopped lean ham, two tablespoonfuls of milk, a quarter of a teaspoon of mixed herbs, a small half-teaspoonful of made mustard, and salt and pepper to taste. Grease four ramekin cases well, fill them rather more than three-quarters full with the mixture, and bake until it is set [about twenty minutes at Mark 4 or 350°F (180°C)]. Then pile on roughly the stiffly whisked white of egg, seasoned with a little salt, and put back in the oven for the egg white to crisp and lightly brown.

LITTLE HAM LOAVES

¼ lb grated lean ham
1 lb mashed potatoes
1 oz butter
2 beaten eggs
Grated nutmeg, chopped parsley, optional
Salt and pepper

Breakfasts or picnics are both equally well served by these little ham loaves. Cook and mash a pound of potatoes and mix them with a quarter of a pound of grated lean ham, an ounce of butter, two beaten eggs, salt and pepper. Grated nutmeg and chopped parsley can be added, either or both, if you care to do so. Mould the mixture into little loaves and fry them, or bake them in the oven, in the latter case gilding them with beaten egg. [They will take about half an hour in a medium oven Mark 4 or 350°F (180°C).] Serve hot for breakfast or lunch, cold for picnics. They are not too hammy in these cold-ham-and-salad days.
[These ham loaves could equally well be moulded into patty shapes by those of us who are not so dexterous.]

HOME-MADE PÂTÉ DE FOIE GRAS

1 lb chicken livers or 2 lb goose livers
¼ lb fat bacon

Sprig thyme
1 bayleaf
1 tablespoon sherry or brandy
Little cream
Salt and pepper
Melted butter

This elegant extra is a tip for the picnic-goers and the high-class tea-party givers. It is a home-made pâté de foie gras. Do not conjure up visions of fatted geese breathing out their last on your lawn. This is a substitute, but in certain circumstances it might not be detected. You want a pound of chicken livers or two of goose livers, and a quarter of a pound of fat bacon. Cut up the latter into small pieces and fry them slowly in a frying-pan. Add the livers cut up small, a sprig of thyme and a bayleaf. Throw in a tablespoonful of sherry or brandy, cook for ten minutes, take out the herbs and pound [the liver] in a mortar. Then pass the mixture through a very fine sieve [or blend it], and mix it with a little cream, salt and pepper. Press down into little pots and when it is quite cold, pour a little melted butter over each.

If you have the heart to deceive your friends, this is an excellent way of doing it, and if you are discovered, then the merit of making this excellent pâté is blushingly yours.

COUNTRY PÂTÉ

2 lb veal [from the shoulder or the knuckle]
1 lb streaky pork
¼ lb calf's or lamb's liver
1 chopped shallot
Parsley
Salt and pepper
Pinch mixed spice
3–4 rashers of streaky bacon
1 bayleaf

B

This is a pâté—or more precisely a terrine, which is only a pâté
without its crust—which would go down well at an early picnic,
or indeed anywhere. Buy two pounds of veal (from which you
should put away a few thin slices), a pound of streaky pork, and a
quarter of a pound of calf's or lamb's liver. Chop and mince these
all finely together with a chopping-knife, and mix them with a
chopped shallot, a little parsley, plenty of salt and pepper, and
some mixed spice. Put a layer of this mince in a buttered terrine
(having first laid a bayleaf at the bottom) then a thin rasher of
bacon (streaky), then a seasoned slice of veal, a rasher, more mince,
and so on till the terrine is full, a rasher of bacon being on the top.
Cover with buttered greaseproof paper, and cook it for an hour
and a quarter in a moderate oven [Mark 4 or 350°F (180°C)].
When it is done, put a weight on top and let it get cold. It will be
all the better if it remains there for at least twenty-four hours
before you want to eat it. And do not forget to see that it is well
seasoned and spiced.

TERRINE OF HARE

    1 lb hare's meat
    1 lb fresh lean pork
    5 oz fat bacon
    6–7 rashers of pickled pork
    A few juniper berries, optional
    Salt and pepper
    1 bayleaf, optional

This is a very simple and useful terrine. You will need a pound of
hare's meat and a pound of fresh lean pork. Chop them both up as
finely as you can with five ounces of fat bacon, adding plenty of
pepper and a little salt. Butter the terrine and lay at the bottom
two or three rashers of pickled pork which have been lightly fried.
Now wrap more thin slices of pickled pork round the mixture of
hare and pork, cover the whole with buttered paper and cook in

the oven for a couple of hours. Put it in a cool place for a night or two before eating it. If you like you can add a few crushed juniper berries to the mixture before potting it, or some grated truffles. Many French cooks demand that a bayleaf should be put at the bottom of the terrine before the pickled pork slices are put in, and there is a good deal to be said for that, too.

[I would recommend cooking this terrine in a baine-marie in a slow to moderate oven, Mark 3 or 4, 325–350°F (170–180°C).]

ANCHOIADE

½ tin anchovies
1 clove of garlic
3 tablespoons olive oil
Dash of vinegar
Pepper
A few breadcrumbs
Bread for toasting

A dish from Provence for garlic lovers. Wash several anchovies and soak them in cold water to remove some of their saltiness. Bone them and mash them with a fork. Now make a sauce with a pounded clove of garlic, a little pepper, three tablespoonfuls of olive oil and a dash of vinegar. Add the anchovies and make a smooth purée of the whole. Thicken, if necessary, with a few breadcrumbs, and spread it on pieces of stale bread, or on toasts, pressing it well down on them so that the sauce sinks in. Then either grill them or bake them in the oven till they are brown. Serve very hot.

POTTED SHRIMPS ON TOAST

[To prepare the shrimps if they are uncooked, first boil them for 3–4 minutes, allow them to cool and then shell them.]

1 pt [boiled] shelled shrimps
4 oz melted butter

Blade of mace
Cayenne pepper
A little grated nutmeg if liked
Clarified butter [see page 32]

First to pot the shrimps. Get a pint of shelled shrimps, and put them into a saucepan with the butter melted, a blade of mace pounded up, as much cayenne as your palate dictates and, if you care for them rather highly spiced, a little grated nutmeg. Heat them up rather slowly with the butter and spices, but on no account let them come to the boil. When they are very hot, pour them into little pots or glasses, let them get cold and then cover them with clarified butter.

Use these shrimps as you like on pieces of toast, simply warming them up but not serving them too hot. (They are, of course, magnificent when cold for breakfast, luncheon, dinner, supper, picnics or in the middle of the night!)

CAULIFLOWER WITH SHRIMPS

1 large cauliflower
Mayonnaise
Picked [boiled] shrimps or prawns

A delicious dish that hails from Belgium. Boil or steam your cauliflower, keeping it whole and being careful that it is not over-cooked and will not fall to pieces. You can test it by gently feeling it with a fork until it is tender. Drain it when done, and leave it to get cold. Stand it upright on a dish, cover it with mayonnaise, and garnish with plenty of picked shrimps, or if you like prawns cut in small pieces. You can add, if you wish, some prettily cut cold carrot and gherkins and some cooked peas; but in my opinion it is better with the shrimps alone.

SMOKED HADDOCK PUFFS

[A favourite with children!]

1 cooked smoked haddock
2 oz self-raising flour
Salt, cayenne pepper
Chopped parsley
2 beaten eggs
Milk added to the water that the fish was cooked in
   (half and half)
Frying fat

Flake up finely the flesh of a cooked smoked haddock, and add a couple of ounces of self-raising flour, a seasoning of salt, cayenne pepper and chopped parsley, two beaten eggs and enough milk and the water the fish was cooked in, half and half, to make a mixture of the same consistency as the batter for a sponge sandwich. Drop tablespoons of this into very hot deep fat, but only two or three at a time, so as to give them plenty of room to puff up.

POTTED SPRATS

[Sprats are delicious little fish and terribly underrated. They are very cheap and need no preparation such as skinning or boning. For a quick meal you can't beat them dipped in flour, fried in butter and served with a good squeeze of lemon!]

1½–2 lb sprats
2 bayleaves
Blade of mace
1 chopped onion
Grated nutmeg
Vinegar or vinegar and water to cover
Butter

Rather more elegant than herrings or mackerel. Take off the heads
and tails, dry them and put them into a fireproof dish. Sprinkle
them with salt and pepper, and add two bayleaves, a blade of
mace, a chopped onion, and a little grated nutmeg. Pour over the
fish enough vinegar or vinegar diluted with water, to cover
them, add one or two small bits of butter, and bake in a moderate
oven [Mark 4 or 350°F (180°C)], covered with a buttered paper,
for about half an hour.

POTATOES FLORENTINE

    I lb spinach
    1½ lb potatoes
    ¼ pt cream [single or double or a mixture of the two]
    Grated cheese

Cook some spinach in the usual way, leaving it in the leaf. Boil the
potatoes (as waxy as possible), peel them and cut them in thin
slices. Arrange some of these in a buttered shallow fireproof dish
on a layer of spinach which you have anointed with some fresh
cream; then season fairly liberally with grated cheese and finally
with a little more cream. Continue to layer finishing with some
cheese on top. Bake in the oven [Mark 5 or 375°F (190°C)] for
about quarter of an hour when the top will be browned.

STUFFED BABY PUMPKINS

[The pumpkin that Ambrose Heath refers to in this recipe is called
squash in greengrocers' shops and comes in various sizes. Marrows,
courgettes, pumpkins and squash are all part of the same family.]

    Small pumpkins (or marrows)—I per person depending on
        size
    I tin tunny [tuna] fish
    Pinch grated Parmesan
    Pinch allspice

Pepper
1 oz butter or margarine
Tomato sauce [see page 127]

Get some very small pumpkins or round marrows (about the size
of a tennis ball or a bit larger), scoop out their insides, and fill with
a mixture of chopped tunney fish (in oil), a pinch of grated Par-
mesan cheese, a little of the flesh of the pumpkin, and a pinch of
pepper and powdered allspice. Cook them slowly in butter or
margarine in a casserole or a baking-dish in the oven [Mark 3 or
325°F (170°C)], and when they are done, they will take about an
hour, serve them with tomato sauce.

LEEK PANCAKE

[I suggest making two pancakes with this mixture as one large one
would be difficult to handle. These quantities would serve two as
a lunch dish or as a side dish.]

1 egg
½ pt milk
4 oz plain flour
4–5 leeks
Butter
Chopped parsley
Salt, pepper
Nutmeg

Make an ordinary pancake batter with the flour, egg and milk, and
while it is resting, stew four or five leeks, the white part only,
and when they are done, chop them up and mix them with the
batter, adding a dessertspoonful of chopped parsley and a seasoning
of salt, pepper and if you like it, nutmeg, but very little of this.
Fry a large pancake on both sides of this mixture, and when it is
dished, sprinkle it with more chopped parsley.

STUFFED TOMATOES

There are so many well-known ways of preparing this savoury that I will content myself with giving one fashion which may be new to some. Tunny [tuna] fish mixed with the pulp of the tomato and seasoned with fresh herbs. This is especially recommended.

TOMATOES WITH SCRAMBLED EGGS

A thick tomato purée made with 1 lb tomatoes
4–5 eggs depending on size
Salt, pepper and a pinch of sugar

One of the most delicious dishes there is, but many people make the mistake, as I think it is, of mixing the tomato with the egg and scrambling it all together. The proper way is to make a thick tomato purée with stewed tomatoes, to season it well with salt, a pinch of sugar and plenty of black pepper, and then to scramble the eggs separately. As soon as the eggs are done, make a wall of them in a very hot dish, pour the tomato purée quickly in the centre, sprinkle instantly with chopped parsley, and serve at once.

EGGS À LA TRIPE

[This is lovely served simply with a plain fresh green salad and can be stretched indefinitely. Allow two onions for every three eggs, and flour and milk in proportion.]

4 sliced onions
6 eggs, hard-boiled
1 tablespoon flour
$\frac{1}{2}$–$\frac{3}{4}$ pt milk
Salt, pepper, nutmeg
Butter

Eggs for luncheon are always nice, eggs à la tripe especially so. Cook the sliced onions in butter till they are soft, add flour and enough milk to make a thick creamy sauce, and season it with salt, pepper and a little grated nutmeg. Into this sauce put halves, quarters or rings of hard-boiled eggs, and serve piping hot.

SORREL OMELETTE

2 eggs per person, modified to 6 eggs for 4 people
A handful of sorrel leaves
Clove garlic
A little chervil

Wash and dry a handful of sorrel leaves, and cut them up finely with a sharp knife. Do not cook it, as some do in making an omelette, but chop a very little garlic and a trifle of chervil and mix this and the sorrel with the beaten eggs. Then cook the omelette in the usual way.

Sorrel, by the way, is perfectly easy to grow if you get one of the large-leaved varieties, which any seedsman should have. These do not seed themselves so rampantly as the meadow sort, and besides they have a less acid flavour.

OMELETTE GRAND'MÈRE

2 eggs per person, modified to 6 for 4 people
Fried cubes of bread
Parsley

This omelette, which is all the nicer for the crunchiness of the fried bread, is made by adding to the eggs before they are cooked some chopped parsley and tiny cubes of very well-fried bread.

OMELETTE CHARTRES

2 eggs per person, modified to 6 for 4 people
Tarragon

Those who especially like the flavour of tarragon will make this unusual omelette by mixing with the eggs some chopped tarragon to their taste. When the omelette is made, it can be decorated prettily with whole tarragon leaves, which must first have been blanched in boiling water; but the decoration must be done quickly, or the omelette will spoil.

SPINACH SOUFFLÉ

½ pt spinach purée
2 eggs plus 1 white
Salt, pepper, nutmeg
Grated cheese

This is an Italian fashion of spinach soufflé. Make half a pint of spinach purée, seasoning it with salt, pepper and a little grated nutmeg. Put it in a small saucepan, add the yolks of two eggs and stir over the fire until the mixture thickens. Let it get cold, then add lightly the stiffly whipped whites of three eggs. It is best to use little soufflé cases [or ramekins] for this, and they should be baked for about ten minutes in a moderate oven [Mark 5 or 375°F (190°C)]. A very little finely grated cheese might be strewn on the top of each [before baking].

MACARONI

1 lb macaroni
1 shallot
1 clove garlic
3 boned anchovy fillets
4 stoned black olives
Olive oil

Cook the macaroni in boiling salted water for about twenty minutes or until it is done, and keep it hot in the saucepan, covered. Chop up very finely a shallot, a small bit of garlic, three boned anchovy fillets (or failing these, add some anchovy essence at the end), and four stoned olives. Put these into a saucepan with a spoonful or two of olive oil, and when the shallot and garlic begin to brown pour all into the drained macaroni, and shake over the heat for a minute or two before serving.

CROÛTE FROMAGÉE

[This is one of the best 'emergency' dishes that I know as the ingredients are usually readily available, unlike the spare tins of salmon or asparagus the perfect hostess is recommended to have in her store cupboard!]

> About 8 slices of ½-inch thick bread
> Enough milk to soak
> Grated cheese, about 4–6 oz
> Margarine or butter

Grease a fireproof dish and arrange in it some half-inch thick slices of bread which have first been soaked in warm milk. See that the slices fit together to cover the bottom.

Now cover them with a layer of grated cheese seasoned with salt and pepper, making this layer half an inch thick as well, or nearly so. Now add one more layer of soaked bread, and one more of cheese, adding just a little more milk to prevent the pudding from drying. Dot with a few thin shavings of butter, and bake very slowly for about half an hour [at Mark 3 or 325°F (170°C)], when the bread should be crisp and the cheese all melted.

CHEESE WAFERS

> Unsweetened ice cream wafers
> Cheese
> Salt and pepper

If you want to serve the cheese course in an amusing way, or are looking for a cheesy something for a picnic, buy some unsweetened wafers. A sandwich of these with peppered and salted cream cheese between them is delicious. And if you wanted to use other cheeses, these can always be used as a filling if you pound them up with some butter in the proportions you like. Roquefort cheese mixed with butter in this way is particularly good, but you must remember that it is rather strong and will want more butter than cheese. But be certain that the wafers are unsweetened, or the novelty will turn out to be a very unamusing one.

CAMEMBERT IN ASPIC

[Camembert treated in this way looks very pretty and could be the *pièce de résistance* at a lunch party.]

Select a fairly ripe Camembert cheese and scrape it lightly. Now choose a tin larger than the cheese, fill it to the depth of an inch with liquid aspic [to make the aspic follow the directions on a packet], and let the jelly set. Then put in the cheese and surround and cover it with more jelly. Let it set—on ice if possible—then :urn it out and serve with sprigs of watercress. You can do cream cheese in the same way.

FRIED CAMEMBERT

This is an acquired taste, but you should set about acquiring it. Get an unripe Camembert cheese, and cut it (having first removed the rind) into long lozenge-shaped pieces. Egg-and-breadcrumb these twice, and fry them in hot fat. Drain well before serving.

Substantial Meals

Lamb and Apricot Stew · Lamb Barbecued · Jugged Lamb · Lamb en Brochette · Leg of Mutton à la Bretonne · Mutton and Beans · Veal with Sour Cream · Veal Stufatino · Veal Cutlets with Cucumber · Kidneys au Vin Blanc · Kidneys with Horseradish · Liver with Olives and Apples · Liver, Fried (French Style) · Sweetbreads, Braised · Tripe à la Creole · Beef Stew · Cold Daube of Beef · Beef Loaf with Sour Cream · Pork Chops with Mustard · Pork Chops with Cranberries · Loin of Pork with Prunes · Barbecued Spareribs of Pork · Ham, Baked · Devilled Chicken · Stuffed Chicken en Cocotte · Chicken à la Limousine · Ragout of Fowl · Chicken with Prunes · Guinea-Fowl à la Normande · Duck à la Bordelaise · Boiled Partridge · Pheasant Flamande · Pigeons, Grilled · Wood-Pigeon Ragout · Jugged Rabbit · Baked Savoury Rabbit

LAMB AND APRICOT STEW

[If the lamb has a lot of fat on it, trim some away. I think scrag (neck) is better than breast of lamb here.]

  Scrag end or breast of lamb
  2 breakfastcups dried apricots, soaked for 2 hours,
    reserving the water

  Suet dumplings
  ¼ lb flour
  2 oz chopped suet
  1 teaspoon chopped parsley
  Salt and pepper
  Pinch ground ginger
  Pinch cayenne
  Pinch mixed sweet herbs

Wash the dried apricots, just cover them with cold water and leave them to soak for two hours. Cut up the meat, just cover it with boiling water, put on the lid and simmer for an hour. Add the apricots then, with the water they soaked in, put the lid on again, and go on cooking for another hour, stirring or shaking the pan now and then. Ten minutes before you want to eat the stew, drop in spoonfuls of suet dumpling mixture, cover again and serve when they are done.

Suet dumplings   Mix together a quarter of a pound of flour, two ounces of chopped suet and a teaspoonful of chopped parsley, seasoning them with salt, pepper, a pinch of ground ginger and sweet herbs, and a trifle of cayenne. Bind with a little cold water, shape into very small balls and cook in the stew.

[These suet dumplings are very good in soups, too.]

LAMB BARBECUED

Cold lamb
2 tablespoons melted margarine or butter
¾ tablespoon vinegar
¼ teaspoon dry mustard
Red currant jelly
Salt, pepper, cayenne

Make a sauce with the two tablespoonfuls of melted margarine or
butter, three-quarters of a tablespoonful of vinegar, a quarter of a
teaspoon of dry mustard, and as much red currant jelly as your
taste demands. Season with salt, pepper and cayenne, and let the
slices of cold lamb heat through in it.

JUGGED LAMB

2 lb lamb cutlets
2 onions, quartered
1 tablespoon butter
4 peeled tomatoes
1 tablespoon flour
1 pt stock
Salt and pepper
Celery salt
Juice ½ lemon
1 dessertspoon red currant jelly
Chopped parsley
Small glass port

This is amusing when hares are out of season. Take two pounds of
well-trimmed lamb cutlets, and brown them on both sides in a
tablespoonful of butter in which you have first browned two
quartered onions. Put the cutlets and onions into a casserole and
add four peeled tomatoes, which should not be too large. Brown

a tablespoonful of flour in the fat in which the onions and cutlets have been fried, and add a pint of stock seasoned with salt, pepper and celery salt. Squeeze in the juice of half a small lemon. Pour this sauce into the casserole, cover it closely and bake in the oven for two hours [Mark 3 or 325°F (170°C)]. Ten minutes or so before you want to serve, stir in a dessertspoonful of red currant jelly, some freshly chopped parsley and a small glass of port. Serve in the casserole.

LAMB EN BROCHETTE

¾ lb lean lamb
French salad dressing [page 130]
¼ lb quartered mushrooms
1 lb quartered tomatoes

Cut the lean lamb into one-inch cubes, pour some French salad dressing over them and leave them, covered, for several hours. When ready, dip some quartered mushrooms and quartered un-skinned tomatoes in the dressing and arrange alternately on metal skewers. Grill them for about ten minutes turning the skewers so that they brown evenly.

LEG OF MUTTON À LA BRETONNE

1 leg of mutton [or lamb]
8 oz haricot beans, soaked overnight
2 large onions
Clove garlic
Salt and pepper
Bouquet of parsley, thyme and bayleaf
2 shallots
Little tomato purée or a chopped tomato
Butter

This is an excellent dish of mutton from Brittany. Cook the joint in the oven, allowing twenty minutes to the pound and twenty minutes over. Soak the beans overnight, and in the morning blanch them by bringing to the boil for five minutes. Throw this blanching water away now and cook them in a casserole with hot water to cover, two large onions, a clove of garlic, salt, pepper and a bouquet of parsley, thyme and a bayleaf. In another pan fry in butter the onions which have been cooked with the beans, a few finely chopped shallots and a little tomato purée or a chopped tomato. Let this last cook for some time until it is a creamy purée, then add the juice from the mutton (without the fat) and the beans. Cook a little longer, stirring the beans carefully so that they do not break. Strain the sauce from the beans, which you will now put in a fireproof dish with the leg upon them. Set the dish in a moderate oven [Mark 4 or 350°F (180°C)] for a quarter of an hour. Serve the sauce separately.

MUTTON AND BEANS

    1 lb lean mutton [or lamb]
    2 breakfastcups haricot beans, soaked overnight and cooked
        for 2 hours
    1 tablespoon lard
    2 chopped onions
    1 level tablespoon flour
    Sprig of thyme
    Salt and pepper
    1 chopped tomato, or 1 tablespoon purée
    Clove garlic
    4 rashers salt bacon, or about ¼ lb pickled pork

Get the butcher to cut you up a pound of lean mutton into two-inch squares. First thing in the morning cook 2 breakfastcupfuls of soaked haricot beans for two hours, and when they are nearly done, heat a level tablespoon of lard in a frying-pan, and put the mutton into it, adding two chopped onions. As the meat browns, stir in a

Substantial Meals

level tablespoonful of flour, and add two breakfastcupfuls of the water in which the beans were cooked, with a sprig of thyme, a chopped tomato (or a spoonful of tomato sauce or purée), a clove of garlic and salt and pepper to taste. Cook quickly for twenty minutes while you put a layer of the beans in an earthenware baking-dish. Now cover these with the pieces of mutton, spread the rest of the beans over them, pour over the strained sauce from the mutton, and on top put four rashers of salt bacon or pickled pork, using about a quarter of a pound in all. Now bake, uncovered, in a moderate oven for an hour [Mark 4 or 350°F (180°C)], and serve in the same dish.

VEAL WITH SOUR CREAM

Slices of cold veal, or cold chicken
2 thinly sliced onions
Paprika pepper
Sour cream

This is an excellent way of using up cold veal, or cold chicken for that matter. Melt a little lard in a stewpan, and in it fry some very thinly sliced onions till they are tender but not browned. When they are done, add a good deal of paprika pepper and some salt, and cook a little longer. The onions should look quite pink by now. Now warm up your slices of veal in a little butter, drain them and arrange on a dish. Pour into the onions as much sour cream as you like, the sourer the better, heat it well up and pour this admirable sauce over the veal, serving it with a dryish purée of potatoes.

VEAL STUFATINO

1 lb leg or shin of veal
2 tablespoons olive oil
2 chopped cloves garlic
Sprig rosemary

¼ pt white wine
½ pt tomato pulp made from fresh or tinned tomatoes
Salt and pepper

The well-known dish from Florence. Cut a pound of leg or shin of veal into pieces two inches long. Heat the olive oil in a saucepan, add two chopped cloves of garlic and a sprig of rosemary, and cook for a few minutes. Add the pieces of meat and fry them brown, turning them so that they colour evenly and seasoning them with salt and pepper. Then add a quarter of a pint of white wine and half a pint of tomato pulp. Simmer for about an hour and a half.

VEAL CUTLETS WITH CUCUMBER

4 thin escalopes of veal
3 oz butter
1 cup cream
Salt, pepper, pinch paprika
1 cucumber, boiled in rounds

Cook the escalopes of veal in butter over a medium flame until they are a pale gold colour, and to the butter and veal juices add, after the cutlets have been removed, a good cupful of cream, salt and pepper and a pinch of paprika. Stir this all well together and boil quickly for a few minutes till it thickens, and then add a few pieces of butter off the flame. Now pour this over the veal which you have surrounded with rounds of boiled cucumber. A really marvellous combination of contrasting flavours.

KIDNEYS AU VIN BLANC

6 sheep's kidneys
1 oz butter or margarine
1 teaspoon flour
½ pt stock

2 tablespoonfuls pale sherry
Salt, and pepper

Skin and cut the sheep's kidneys into thin slices, and brown them
quickly in a little butter or margarine. Add the flour, mix in, then
season with salt and pepper and moisten with the stock and a
spoonful or two of pale sherry. Cook together for a few minutes
only, then serve at once.

KIDNEYS WITH HORSERADISH

6 sheep's kidneys or 8 lambs' kidneys
Butter, margarine or olive oil
Grated horseradish

Grill the kidneys by slitting across without actually cutting in half,
take out the core, and skewer them open flat with little skewers,
one or more on a skewer according to the eater's capacity. Dip
them in melted butter or margarine or olive oil, and grill them for
eight minutes, turning them frequently. Fill them with grated
horseradish, and serve them with fried potatoes.

LIVER WITH OLIVES AND APPLES

1 large onion, chopped
Butter
A few stoned olives [I prefer black, but you can use green]
4 rashers of bacon, diced
1 lb liver, any variety
Flour
Salt and pepper
3 eating apples, cored and peeled and poached in water until
    soft, in quarters

An unusual way of cooking liver is the following. Chop up an
onion and fry it in butter till brown. Stone and chop a few olives,

and fry them with the bacon, and some salt and pepper, for a few minutes longer. Meanwhile in another pan, fry in butter or bacon fat some pieces of liver which have been rolled in flour and seasonings. Dish the liver, sprinkle the onions and olives over them, and surround them with some well-drained quarters of cored and peeled apples which have been poached in water till tender.

LIVER, FRIED (FRENCH STYLE)

[I have cooked liver in this way for numerous people who swear that they dislike the taste of liver and they have been converted by this dish. Lemon squeezed over it is delicious.]

Liver
Egg beaten up and breadcrumbs
Deep fat
Parsley

The liver is cut into thin strips (*aiguillettes*) egg-and-breadcrumbed [that is, dipped first in egg and then in breadcrumbs], and fried in deep fat. They are served in a heap, garnished with fried parsley.

SWEETBREADS, BRAISED

2 pairs of calves' or 1 lb lambs' sweetbreads
1 small onion
1 small carrot
½ small turnip
1 stick celery
½ dozen white peppercorns
A bouquet of parsley, thyme and bayleaf
½ pt stock

First blanch the sweetbreads by putting them in a saucepan with enough cold water to cover them completely, and bring to the boil gently. Let them boil for ten minutes; withdraw them and plunge them into a basin of fresh water. Dry on a clean cloth and remove as much skin and membrane as possible.

Cut up a small onion, a small carrot, half a small turnip, and a stick of celery, and put them into a stewpan just big enough for the sweetbreads, adding half a dozen peppercorns, a bouquet of parsley, thyme and bayleaf, and enough stock to cover the vegetables. Wrap the sweetbreads in buttered paper, lay them on the vegetables, put on the lid, and cook gently for three-quarters of an hour. [Unwrap the sweetbreads and serve with the vegetables.]

TRIPE À LA CREOLE

2 lb tripe
2 sliced onions
1 tablespoon butter
1 oz lean ham, chopped fine
2 cloves garlic
3 sprigs thyme
3 bayleaves, finely chopped
12 large ripe tomatoes, or a 2 lb tin
Cayenne pepper and salt

Boil two pounds of tripe until tender, about an hour and a half, and then cut it into slices about two inches long and half an inch wide. Now stew a couple of finely sliced onions with a tablespoon of butter in a closed stewpan, and when soft add a square inch of lean ham chopped very fine. Add also two finely chopped cloves of garlic, and three sprigs of thyme and three bayleaves also finely chopped. Finally, put in twelve large ripe tomatoes or the contents of a two-pound tin of them. If you use fresh tomatoes, peel them first. Season with salt and cayenne pepper, and cook for ten minutes. Now add the pieces of tripe, put on the lid closely, and cook gently for another twenty-five minutes. Serve very hot.

BEEF STEW

1½ lb stewing steak [if it has a lot of fat on it trim it a little
  but not too much or the beef will lose flavour]
2 sliced onions
Bacon bones, or some pieces of fattish bacon
½ teacup vinegar
1 dessertspoon black treacle
1 bottle mild ale and an equal quantity of water
2 cloves
½ bayleaf, salt, pepper

Get a piece of stewing steak about a pound and a half in weight,
flatten it well, roll it up and tie it. Put a few bits of fattish bacon, or
even some bacon bones, into a stewpan with a few sliced onions,
put the beef on top, and just cover it with a mixture of half a
teacupful of vinegar, a dessertspoon of black treacle and equal
parts of mild ale and water. Season with salt, pepper, one or two
cloves and half a bayleaf, cover closely and cook gently, preferably
in the oven, for about three hours. [Oven temperature Mark 3 or
325°F (170°C).]

COLD DAUBE OF BEEF

3 lb fillet of beef
1 lb finely chopped pork, ½ lb fat and ½ lb lean
4 onions
Parsley
4–5 shallots
Bacon rashers, about ½ lb
½ lb carrots
A few veal bones
A bouquet of parsley, thyme, bayleaf
Salt and pepper
Grated nutmeg

    1 cup water
    Glass dry white wine
    1 tablespoon tomato purée

Make a mixture of a pound of finely chopped pork (fat and lean in equal parts), two onions, some parsley and a few shallots, and season them with salt, pepper and spices. Cut three pounds of fillet of beef into thin slices, and beat them flat. Put down a slice and on it a layer of the pork mixture, and then enough rashers of bacon to cover it. Continue to do this until it is all used up, finishing with a slice of beef, and tie the piece up. In a fireproof dish prepare a bed of sliced carrots and onions, a few veal bones and a bouquet of parsley, thyme and a bayleaf; season with salt, pepper and a little nutmeg; lay the beef on this and pour over it a cup of water, a glass of dry white wine and a tablespoonful of tomato purée. Put on the lid, and cook slowly in the oven for at least four hours. When it is done, the beef may be placed in a deep dish, and the gravy (which will make a lovely jelly) strained over it. It should stand for at least a day before being eaten. [Oven temperature Mark 2 or 300°F (150°C).]

BEEF LOAF WITH SOUR CREAM

    $\frac{1}{2}$ lb beef
    $\frac{1}{2}$ lb pork
    1 small white roll
    Milk to soak bread in
    Salt and pepper
    1 egg
    Fresh breadcrumbs
    1 small carton sour cream
    Fat or dripping to baste

Soak a small dinner roll in milk, squeeze it as dry as you can, and put it through a mincing machine with half a pound of beef and

half a pound of pork. Season with salt and pepper, and bind with
a beaten egg or an egg yolk. Shape into a loaf, brush it over with
white of egg, and sprinkle with breadcrumbs. Now put it into a
greased baking-tin, pour a little boiling fat over it and bake it in
the oven [Mark 4 or 350°F (180°C)] for about three-quarters of an
hour, basting it alternately with its own fat and with sour cream,
the combination of which will make a pleasant sauce to serve with
it when the loaf is browned.

PORK CHOPS WITH MUSTARD

4–5 pork chops
Sprinkling of flour
1 teaspoon dry mustard
1 teaspoon vinegar
1 teacup water
Small carton sour cream
Salt

Rub four or five pork chops well with salt, grill quickly on each
side until brown, then sprinkle them with flour and put them in a
baking-tin. Mix together a small teaspoonful of mustard, a teaspoonful of vinegar and a teacupful of water, and then when it is
smoothly mixed, pour it over the chops. Cook for a quarter of an
hour in a hot oven [Mark 6 or 400°F (200°C)], then pour over
them some sour cream and a dash of salt, and bake for another ten
minutes, basting twice.

PORK CHOPS WITH CRANBERRIES

4–5 pork chops
1 breakfastcup minced cranberries
2 tablespoons honey
Pinch of ground cloves
Salt

Brown the pork chops quickly on both sides, sprinkle them with salt and put them in a baking-dish. Cover them with the cranberries, the honey and the ground cloves mixed. Cover and bake in a moderate oven [Mark 4 or 350°F (180°C)] for about an hour.

LOIN OF PORK WITH PRUNES

3 lb piece of loin of pork
½ lemon
2 oz prunes
Salt
A little cream

Rub a three-pound piece of loin of pork with half a lemon until there is no juice left. Parboil the prunes [reserving the juice], stone them and cut them in four. Make close rows of holes in the loin with a skewer and stuff each with a piece of prune. Grease a baking-tin, put in the loin, and let it brown in a hot oven, then sprinkle with salt, and pour over it the hot liquid from the prunes' cooking. Then roast in a moderate oven, basting it every ten minutes. [Allow twenty minutes to the pound and twenty minutes over, starting it off at Mark 7 or 425°F (220°C) for the first 15 minutes and then Mark 6 or 400°F (200°C) for the rest of the cooking time.]

BARBECUED SPARERIBS OF PORK

2 lb spareribs [Chinese spareribs can also be used]
⅓ breakfastcup water
3 teacups vinegar
⅓ breakfastcup melted butter
⅓ breakfastcup chilli sauce [see page 123]
2 tablespoons grated horseradish
2 tablespoons Worcester sauce
½ teaspoon salt
Pinch cayenne pepper

Grill the spareribs very slowly for half an hour, when the joint should be crisp and brown. While it is cooking, baste it now and then with the following sauce. Mix and heat together a third of a breakfastcupful of water, three smaller cupfuls of vinegar, a third of a breakfastcupful each of melted butter and chilli sauce, the grated horseradish, the Worcester sauce, salt and cayenne pepper. When the joint is cooked serve this sauce with it.

HAM, BAKED

[A corner of gammon is a suitably small joint for a family meal. They usually weigh about 3–6 lb and may be cooked in the same way as a larger ham.]
After the ham has been scrubbed well with a stiff brush it is placed, fat side upwards, in a baking-tin and baked in a slow oven [Mark 2 or 300°F (150°C)]. Allow twenty-five minutes to the pound for a ten-to-twelve-pound ham, and for larger ones twenty minutes to the pound; and three-quarters of an hour before it is done, take it from the oven, remove the rind and either spread it with one of the following mixtures, or baste it during the cooking time as suggested below.

Spreadings (1) A breakfastcupful of brown sugar moistened with some of the drippings. (2) A breakfastcupful of brown sugar mixed with three level dessertspoonfuls of flour or half a teacupful of fine breadcrumbs. (3) A breakfastcupful of brown sugar moistened with three dessertspoonfuls of vinegar, cider or fruit juice. (4) A breakfastcupful of brown sugar mixed with a level teaspoon of mustard and three teaspoons or so of vinegar, enough to make a spreadable paste.

Bastings (1) Cider, champagne, pineapple juice, mixed fruit juices or strained honey. (2) Maple syrup. (3) The juice of an orange and of a lemon and a breakfastcupful of sugar cooked together for five minutes.

DEVILLED CHICKEN

1 small chicken or 2 or more poussins
Olive oil
Salt, pepper, ground ginger
Chopped parsley
A little chopped onion

An attractive Italian version. Poussins or small chicken are best for this dish. Cut them down the back, flatten and skewer them. Sprinkle them with plenty of olive oil, seasoning them with salt, pepper and ground ginger (but not too much of the last) and then sprinkle them with chopped parsley and onion. Leave them in this marinade for an hour, turning them once. Then grill them, and serve them as hot as possible.

STUFFED CHICKEN EN COCOTTE

1 chicken, weighing about 3½ lb
3 small onions
6 sliced mushrooms
Chicken's liver
2 rashers of bacon
Butter, the size of an egg
6 potatoes
A few artichoke bottoms
Stock and a little white wine
Salt and pepper

First make a stuffing by frying in butter for five minutes the small onions cut in slices. When they are getting brown, take them out and put in half a dozen sliced mushrooms. Cook these for a few minutes. Chop up the liver of the chicken (or two if you can get another), and mix it with the mushrooms and onions. Stuff the chicken with this mixture.

Cook, in a cocotte large enough to hold the chicken, a couple of rashers of bacon with a piece of butter the size of an egg. When the bacon is cooked, take it out and brown the chicken in the butter, turning it on all sides. Now put back the bacon and add half a dozen potatoes cut in thin slices and some artichoke bottoms quartered. Cook all together without a lid for half an hour. Then take everything out of the cocotte except the gravy, pour in a small quantity of good stock and white wine, and let it reduce a little [on top of the stove]. Season, put back the chicken and the other ingredients and serve as it is. No other vegetables are needed with this admirable dish. If you do not like the taste of wine, leave it out.

CHICKEN À LA LIMOUSINE

1 chicken, weighing about 3½ lb
24 chestnuts
¼ lb sausage meat
Chopped parsley
2 onions
Stick celery
Approximately ½ pt stock
Pinch of salt and sugar
Butter

Peel a couple of dozen chestnuts [see page 24 on how to peel], and cook them on a slow fire for half an hour in a casserole just large enough to hold them. In the casserole should also be a small stick of celery, a piece of butter the size of a walnut, a pinch of salt and sugar and enough stock to cover the contents. While this is cooking, make a stuffing of a quarter of a pound of sausage meat, chopped parsley and two onions chopped up and lightly cooked in butter. Having stuffed the chicken with this mixture, brown it quickly on all sides in butter and then cook it for twenty minutes in the oven in a casserole with the lid off. Add the chestnuts then and the strained sauce in which they have been cooking, and continue to cook until the chicken is done. [Oven temperature Mark 4 or 350°F (180°C).]

RAGOUT OF FOWL

[Boiling fowl are usually fairly large birds, but they are very inexpensive compared to roasting chickens and ideal for feeding a large number of people. When they are cooked slowly and for a long time I think they have an unbeatable flavour that is rarely found in today's pre-packaged frozen birds.]

    1 jointed boiling fowl
    3 rashers of bacon
    1 onion, finely chopped
    ½ bottle red wine
    1 pt water
    1 tablespoon flour
    4 bruised cloves garlic
    Bouquet of parsley, thyme, bayleaf
    Mushrooms, optional
    Salt and pepper

If an old boiling fowl should come your way, it can be appetizingly disguised in the following manner, if you will not begrudge half a bottle of inexpensive red wine. Fry the bacon with the chopped onions in a casserole until the onion is just turning colour, and add to them the cut-up fowl. Let the pieces stew gently for a while, then stir in a good spoonful of flour and moisten with half a bottle of red wine and a pint of water. Add four bruised cloves of garlic, a bouquet of parsley, thyme and a bayleaf, salt and pepper, and cook slowly till the flesh is ready to drop from the bones, for two or three hours according to the age of the bird. A few mushrooms can be added with advantage if liked. [Oven temperature Mark 3 or 325°F (170°C).]

CHICKEN WITH PRUNES

1 3½–4 lb chicken
1 oz butter or margarine
3 bacon rashers, finely chopped, plus at least 4 rashers of
  streaky cut in half
3 small onions, diced
3 small carrots, diced
At least 8 soaked prunes

In the bottom of the baking-dish in which you have melted a good piece of butter or margarine put a bed of finely chopped bacon rashers mixed with three small onions and three small carrots cut in tiny dice. Put the chicken on these, and roast in a moderate oven [Mark 4 or 350°F (180°C) for about an hour and a quarter depending on size], basting well. Serve it with a garnish of prunes thus: Soak the prunes, drain, dry and stone them carefully. Wrap each in a piece of thin streaky bacon, and bake them in the oven, turning over and over until the bacon is crisp all round. [The prunes wrapped in bacon will take about fifteen minutes to cook.]

GUINEA-FOWL À LA NORMANDE

Guinea-fowl
1 lb apples
Small carton cream [double if possible]
Butter

Guinea-fowl is inclined to be rather a dull bird unless he is dressed a little, and this fashion from Normandy (it is mostly applicable to pheasant or chicken) will do very well for a change. Fry the guinea-fowl in a casserole in butter till he is browned lightly, and meanwhile toss a few peeled, cored and finely-chopped apples in a little butter, too. Put a layer of apple in the bottom of the casserole, the guinea-fowl on top, and put the rest of the apples round him.

Pour over a few spoonfuls of cream, and cook in the oven with the lid on for about half an hour or until the guinea-fowl is done. Serve in the casserole. It is an admirable surprise. [Oven temperature Mark 5 or 375°F (190°C).]

DUCK À LA BORDELAISE

    1 4 lb duck—keep the liver
    2 oz mushrooms
    ½ oz butter
    3–4 chopped black olives
    1 large tablespoon stale white breadcrumbs soaked in a
        little milk and then pressed dry
    1 beaten egg
    A little parsley
    A little chopped garlic
    Salt and pepper

One of the best ways of stuffing a duck, as experience will show: Toss some minced mushrooms in a little butter, and mix these with a few chopped olives, some parsley, a faintest touch of chopped garlic, the liver of the duck, and some stale breadcrumbs soaked in milk and then pressed dry. Season the mixture rather highly, and bind it with a beaten egg. A duck thus stuffed and roasted demands no more than its own delicious gravy.

[To roast the duck, first wipe the bird and rub it all over with salt, prick it well all over with a fork, and put it in a roasting tin with a little water. Allow twenty minutes per pound and roast in a moderate oven, Mark 4 or 350°F (180°C).]

BOILED PARTRIDGE

Lest anyone think this is sacrilege, let them first try one of the most exquisite, if not the most exquisite dishes of partridge to be discovered anywhere.

2 partridges, to serve 4
8 vine leaves
½ lb thin rashers fat bacon
Water
Salt

See that they are young birds and salt them inside and out. Wrap them well first in vine leaves and then in thin rashers of fat bacon. Boil them in plain unsalted water for thirty-five minutes, take them out and at once (this is important) plunge them into iced water, where they must remain until cold, but no longer. Unwrap them to serve. In this way you have nothing but the true and perfect flavour of the best of game.

PHEASANT FLAMANDE

[Pheasants should be well basted during cooking. A medium-sized pheasant will take about an hour to cook in a moderate oven Mark 4 or 350°F (180°C). A young bird will take less time, about thirty to forty minutes. Rub the bird with butter before putting it into the roasting-tin.]

1 pheasant
2 lb sauerkraut
1 lb chipolata sausages
A little pork fat
3–4 rashers of thin streaky bacon
6 dried juniper berries
A few slices of garlic-flavoured salami
¼ pt dry white wine
Salt and pepper

A dish for those who like sauerkraut. Roast the pheasant in the usual way, and when it is done, bury it in the sauerkraut and cook for twenty minutes in a slow oven [Mark 2 or 300°F (150°C)], serving with grilled chipolata sausages round it and its own gravy

C

poured over it. The sauerkraut is prepared thus: Wash and drain well two pounds of it. Rub a deep pan with pork fat, and put in the sauerkraut with a few pieces of thin streaky bacon, half a dozen dried juniper berries coarsely broken, a few slices of garlic-flavoured salami, salt, pepper and a quarter of a pint of dry white wine. Put on the lid and cook in a slow oven [Mark 2 or 300°F (150°C)] for three hours.

PIGEONS, GRILLED

[These pigeons must be very young if they are to be grilled.]

> 2 pigeons—1 between two people
> Butter or margarine
> Breadcrumbs—dried white

Halve and flatten the pigeons, brush them over with melted butter or margarine, and roll them in breadcrumbs. Grill them gently and serve the following sauce separately.

> *For the sauce*
> 1 rasher bacon
> 2 shallots
> 1 small onion
> 2 peeled mushrooms
> 1½ oz butter or margarine
> Bouquet of parsley, thyme and bayleaf
> A drop of vinegar
> 1 sherry-glass dry white wine
> ¼ pt stock
> 1 tablespoonful tomato purée, fresh or tinned concentrated
> 1 oz lean ham
> 2 gherkins
> Parsley
> Cayenne pepper

Chop up the bacon, shallots, small onion and the peeled mushrooms, and stew them gently for a few minutes in the butter or
margarine. Add the bouquet of parsley, thyme and bayleaf, a drop
of vinegar, a sherry-glassful of dry white wine and of stock, a
pinch of cayenne pepper, and a spoonful of tomato purée. Bring
to the boil, let it reduce well until it is as thick as cream. Pass it
through a strainer, put it back into the saucepan, and at the last add
a little lean ham, some parsley and a few gherkins all finely chopped.

WOOD-PIGEON RAGOUT

2 wood-pigeons
2–3 tablespoons olive oil [or vegetable oil]
2 onions
2 carrots
2 sticks celery
1 clove garlic
1 bayleaf, a little parsley, sage, rosemary and thyme
2 glasses red wine
1 glass vinegar [French wine vinegar is best]
1 teaspoon anchovy essence
Salt and pepper
Chopped parsley

An excellent Italian fashion. Cut the pigeons up as for a fricassee.
In two or three tablespoonfuls of olive oil brown lightly in a
stewpan the onions, the carrots and two sticks of celery, all
chopped, a clove of garlic, a bayleaf and a little parsley, sage,
rosemary and thyme. Be careful you do not overdo the herbs.
Then add the pigeons, and brown them quickly, adding salt and
pepper. Now add a glass of red wine and the same of vinegar,
cover and simmer very gently until the pigeons are done [about an
hour]. Take out the pieces, and dilute the sauce with a very little
water. Rub the vegetables back into it through a sieve, add a
teaspoonful of anchovy essence, put back the pieces of pigeon,

heating them well through, and serve them sprinkled with
chopped parsley.

JUGGED RABBIT

[A good-sized rabbit weighs approximately 2½ lb and will feed
4–6 people. An amiable butcher will joint it for you or you can
buy separate pieces. Frozen rabbit will need to be defrosted
overnight. A much tastier result will be obtained with a wild
rabbit if you can get it.]

    1 rabbit
    2 sliced onions
    4–5 rashers of bacon
    Salt and pepper

Cut the rabbit in pieces and sprinkle them with salt and pepper.
Slice up two large onions. Take a stewpan with a closely fitting
lid, and put in it a layer of the onion, one of rabbit, then onion,
and so on until the pan is full. Cover the top layer with slices of
bacon, put a piece of paper underneath the lid, and then put this
on tightly. Cook on top of the stove for at least two hours. There
is no need to add any liquid, the rabbit conveniently makes its
own gravy.

BAKED SAVOURY RABBIT

[Make sure that you have enough breadcrumbs, at least ½ lb.]

    1 rabbit weighing about 2 lb
    3–4 boiled chopped onions
    Breadcrumbs, fresh white
    Sage
    2 oz melted margarine or dripping
    Salt and pepper

Make a mixture of three or four boiled and chopped onions, breadcrumbs, sage, salt, pepper and an ounce of melted margarine or dripping. It should be like sage-and-onion stuffing for duck. Melt the rest of the dripping in a fireproof dish, spread half the breadcrumb mixture on this, and arrange the pieces of uncooked rabbit on top. Cover with the rest of the mixture, and bake in a good oven [Mark 5 or 375°F (190°C)], for an hour or an hour and a half. An honest English dish.

Fish

Sole with Spinach · Sole Murat · Shattuck Halibut · Scallops à l'Etouffée · Eels, Cold (Italian Fashion) · Trout Doria · Trout with Chives · Brill with Mustard Sauce · Red Mullet à la Livornaise · Cold Red Mullet à l'Oriental · Salmon Bretonne · Herrings à la Portière · Soused Herrings · Cold Baked Mackerel (Eastern Fashion) · Mackerel en Papillotes · Cold Marinated Mackerel (French Fashion) · Cod à la Creole · Cod in Cider · Baked Sprats · Whitebait · Crab aux Oeufs · Crab Fried in Batter · Mussels à la Catalane · Mussels, Fried · Fish Pancake · Fish Pie with Pastry · Sardines

SOLE WITH SPINACH

1 sole weighing 1¼–1½ lb, filleted
1 lb spinach, cooked
1 minced onion
Breadcrumbs
Butter
Grated cheese, optional

Season and flour the fillets of sole, and cook them in butter until golden. Arrange them round a heap of cooked spinach with which you have mixed some finely minced onion fried separately in butter. Sprinkle some breadcrumbs over the dish, add a little melted butter, and brown quickly in the oven. Grated cheese could be added to the breadcrumbs if liked more savoury, but it is very good as it is.

SOLE MURAT

1 sole weighing 1¼–1½ lb, filleted
Butter
1 lb potatoes, cut in strips
4 artichoke bottoms
Squeeze lemon juice
Chopped parsley
Salt and pepper

Cut the filleted sole diagonally in pieces about the size of a large whitebait, season and flour them and fry them in butter until they are golden. Fry also separately the strips of potatoes and the artichoke bottoms which are also cut in strips, in butter, and when done, mix them all together in the serving dish, and sprinkle with chopped parsley. Some nut-brown butter flavoured with lemon juice is poured over this delightful mixture at the last.

SHATTUCK HALIBUT

[Cod would be good cooked like this.]

  1½ lb halibut
  3 tomatoes, sliced
  2 green peppers, cut into strips
  Melted butter or margarine
  Salt and pepper

Butter a fireproof dish, and lay in it a pound and a half steak of halibut, sprinkling it with salt and pepper, and arranging on the top five or six thick slices of peeled tomato and some very thin strips of green pepper. Bake in a hot oven [Mark 6 or 400°F (200°C)] for half an hour, basting frequently with melted butter or margarine and with the liquid in the dish.

SCALLOPS À L'ÉTOUFFÉE

[Ask the fishmonger to prepare the scallops for you.]

  2 scallops per person
  Mushrooms, allow 3 per scallop
  Lemon juice
  Salt and pepper

Wash and drain the scallops carefully, and put them whole into a buttered saucepan. Now add the peeled and sliced mushrooms, salt, pepper, and a little lemon juice. Do not add any more liquid, but put the lid on firmly, and cook very slowly for twenty-five to thirty minutes. They will make their own sauce. All you have to do now is to put the scallops into the hot shells, add a few slices of mushroom and a little of the sauce, and serve as they are.

EELS, COLD (ITALIAN FASHION)

[There are two varieties of eel that could be used, one is fresh river eel which is more tender but at a price, and the other is conger eel.]

1½ lb eel
Olive oil
½–¾ pt vinegar
3 chilli peppers
Sprigs rosemary

Cut the eels in pieces an inch and a half long, and fry them in deep hot olive oil until light golden. Drain them well on a cloth. In another pan put half to three-quarters of a pint of vinegar, bring to the boil, and add three chilli peppers and a few sprigs of rosemary. Put the eels into a deep dish, and pour the [strained] boiling vinegar over them. They are to be eaten cold.

TROUT DORIA

1 trout per person
Flour
Butter
Lemon juice
Chopped parsley
1 cucumber, peeled and cut in olive shapes

This is a pleasant variant of the *meunière* way of cooking trout. Flour the fish and cook them in a little butter till they are golden on each side. Take them out, keep them warm and continue to cook the butter till it browns slightly. Then squeeze in a little lemon juice, stir together and pour over the fish, which you will garnish with some chopped parsley and the olive-shaped pieces of cucumber which have meanwhile been stewed in butter.

TROUT WITH CHIVES

[You will need half a pint of cream for 4 trout. This is rather extravagant but it is worth it.]

1 trout per person
1 dessertspoon water
Juice of a lemon
Salt and pepper
Chopped parsley
Chopped chives
Double cream for sauce
Breadcrumbs, fresh white

Lay the trout on a thickly buttered dish and add a dessertspoonful of water, the juice of a lemon, salt, pepper, some chopped parsley and plenty of chopped chives. Cook in a moderate oven [Mark 4 or 350°F (180°C)] for ten minutes. Meanwhile, boil as much cream as you want for the sauce. When the cooking time is up, pour this over the trout, sprinkle some breadcrumbs over and brown in the oven.

BRILL WITH MUSTARD SAUCE

1½–2 lb brill
Water to cook in with the addition of salt and a spoonful
  of vinegar
2 tablespoons butter or margarine
½ teaspoon chopped parsley
1 teaspoon lemon juice
2 teaspoons French mustard
1 yolk of egg

Cook the brill in boiling salted water to which you have added a spoonful of vinegar, for a quarter of an hour, then drain it, reserving two spoonfuls of the liquid, and send it to the table with the following sauce. Let two tablespoonfuls of butter or margarine just colour a light brown, then add the two tablespoonfuls of the liquid the fish was cooked in, half a teaspoon of chopped parsley, a teaspoonful of lemon juice, and two teaspoonfuls of

French mustard. When well mixed, stir in the yolk of an egg, and let it cook but not boil.

RED MULLET À LA LIVORNAISE

4 red mullet
4–5 tablespoons olive oil
2 chopped cloves garlic
Handful of chopped parsley
Chopped small stick celery
3–4 large tomatoes
Salt and pepper

This is perhaps the most famous, and certainly the most savoury, way of cooking a delicious fish, which should be either left uncleaned or, better, cleaned but with the liver left in. It is cooked in the following sauce. Put four or five tablespoonfuls of oil into a saucepan, and when it is hot, add two chopped cloves of garlic, a handful of chopped parsley and a small stick of celery also chopped. As soon as the garlic begins to brown, add three or four large chopped tomatoes, season with salt and pepper, and simmer until the tomatoes are a pulp. Rub through a sieve, and cook the fish for about twenty minutes in this sauce, turning once or twice if necessary. Sprinkle with chopped parsley on serving.

COLD RED MULLET À L'ORIENTAL

4 red mullet
1 small, chopped onion
4 tablespoons olive oil
3 tomatoes
Bouquet of parsley, thyme and bayleaf
1 gill white wine, approximately
1 clove garlic
Small tin pimientos, or fresh

    Salt and pepper
    Coriander seeds
    Pinch saffron
    1 lemon

Lightly brown the chopped onion in olive oil, add the roughly chopped tomatoes, a bouquet of parsley, thyme and a bayleaf, a little white wine, a touch of garlic, some chopped sweet red peppers (pimientos) which can be tinned if necessary, salt, pepper, and a little of an infusion of coriander seeds and saffron. Cook for a quarter of an hour, and reduce it. Fry the mullet quickly in very hot olive oil, arrange them well-drained in the serving-dish, cover them with the tomato mixture, let them get cold in it, and serve decorated with thin slices of unpeeled lemon.

SALMON BRETONNE

[An extravagant but excellent dish.]

    1 lb salmon, raw
    Butter or margarine
    1 lb fresh mushrooms, small ones
    Chopped parsley
    Lemon juice

An excellent dish and a change from the usual run of salmon dishes. Cut the raw salmon into cubes of about one-inch sides, and fry them quickly [in an ovenproof dish] in butter or margarine with a few small fresh mushrooms. When half-cooked, put the pan into a moderate oven [Mark 4 or 350°F (180°C)], and let them finish cooking there, then drain them and serve them sprinkled with chopped parsley, lightly browned butter (*beurre noisette*) and a little lemon juice.

HERRINGS À LA PORTIÈRE

1 herring per person
A little milk
Salt and pepper
Flour to coat
Approximately 2 oz butter
Made mustard
Parsley
A little vinegar [wine vinegar would be best]

Here is a way of doing herrings with mustard. Make two or three incisions on each side, and then roll them in a little milk. Season them with salt and pepper and roll them in some flour. Now cook them in butter in a frying-pan till they are golden on each side, then arrange them on a long dish, and with a little brush paint them with made mustard, but not too thickly. Sprinkle them with chopped parsley. Brown a little butter in the pan you have used for the fish, pour this over them, and very quickly swill the pan with a drop of vinegar, and pour this over the butter. Serve very hot indeed.

SOUSED HERRINGS

[Good hot or cold.]

6 herrings
Salt and pepper
1 bayleaf
6 allspice
3 cloves
Pinch ground mace
2 parts vinegar to 1 part water
Onion, optional

Wash half a dozen herrings thoroughly after cleaning them, and take off their heads. Put them in a pie-dish, head-to-tail, sprinkling the layers of fish with salt and pepper. Add the bayleaf, the allspice, the cloves and the pinch of ground mace, and cover them with two parts vinegar to one part water. Some add a little sliced onion. Cover with a buttered paper or a lid and bake in a very slow oven [Mark 2 or 300°F (150°C)] for an hour and a half. These fish will keep for some days if kept submerged and in a cool place, but heat them up very slowly.

COLD BAKED MACKEREL (EASTERN FASHION)

1 mackerel per person
2 sliced onions
1 lb tomatoes to about 4 fish
1–2 lemons
About ½ pt tomato sauce [fresh or tinned tomatoes made into a sauce. See page 127 for recipe]

Mackerel, and other suitable fish, are served cold in the East in this way. If they are very small fish simply clean them and remove their heads and tails; if large, fillet them. Slice some onions finely, and in a well-greased fireproof dish arrange alternate rows of fish and onion, covering with thin slices of tomato and lemon, and finally pouring over some tomato sauce. Bake until the fish is done [about an hour at Mark 3 or 325°F (170°C)], and let it grow cold.

MACKEREL EN PAPILLOTES

1 mackerel per person
Shallots or spring onions
Chopped parsley
Olive oil [corn oil or any vegetable oil would be suitable]
Lemon
Butter
Salt and freshly ground black pepper

This dish comes from Flanders. Keep the mackerel whole, clean them and stuff them with the following butter: Chopped shallots or spring onions, parsley, salt, freshly ground black pepper and lemon juice all combined with the butter. Then butter some pieces of greaseproof paper and wrap each fish in one, twisting the ends together. Brush these paper bags over on the outside with olive oil, and grill or bake them slowly for three-quarters of an hour. The fish should be dished up out of their cases with the cooking butter poured over them. A garnish of quartered lemons may be added.

[I found that slow baking in the oven at Mark 3 or 325°F (170°C) was much easier than grilling.]

COLD MARINATED MACKEREL (FRENCH FASHION)

4 mackerel
2 parts white wine to 1 part vinegar to cover
1 medium onion
1 carrot
2–3 shallots
2 sprigs thyme
Parsley
Bayleaf
Salt and peppercorns

Put two parts of white wine and one part wine vinegar in a [flameproof] earthenware casserole with a medium-sized onion sliced, a sliced carrot, two or three chopped shallots, two sprigs of thyme, parsley, a bayleaf, salt and some peppercorns. Bring to the boil and simmer for twenty minutes. Take off the fire and when the marinade is lukewarm, put in the mackerel and let them poach for a quarter of an hour. Leave in the marinade until they are cold.

COD À LA CREOLE

1½ lb piece of cod
1 tablespoon olive oil
1 tablespoon wine vinegar
Good squeeze of lemon juice
1 tablespoon chopped onion
½ pt tomato purée, made from fresh or tinned tomatoes
½ chopped green pepper, or red
Salt and pepper
Grated cheese

Bone the cod and soak it for half an hour, turning it once or twice, in a tablespoonful of olive oil, the same of vinegar, a good squeeze of lemon juice, and a tablespoonful of chopped onion. Grease a fireproof dish, put in the fish, and pour over it the strained marinade in which it has soaked, with half a pint of tomato purée, a tablespoonful of chopped green pepper, or red pepper would do at a pinch, and a seasoning of salt and pepper. Cover the dish, and bake in a moderate oven [Mark 4 or 350°F (180°C)] for about three-quarters of an hour. When done, sprinkle with a little grated cheese, and brown.

COD IN CIDER

1½ lb cod steak
1 tablespoon olive oil
1 pint dry cider
Salt and pepper
1 oz butter
Little flour
Parsley
A few mushrooms
1 shallot, or onion

In Brittany they have a pleasant way of cooking cod in cider. Skin and bone the cod, and cut it into pieces. Put them into a casserole with a tablespoon of olive oil and a pint of dry cider. Season with salt and pepper. Add a piece of butter about half the size of an egg which you have mixed with a little flour and parsley, shallot (or onion) and mushrooms finely chopped together. Cook all this quickly over the flame, so the fish is done and the sauce suitably reduced at the same time.

BAKED SPRATS

1½–2½ lb sprats
Salt and pepper
Lemon juice
Butter or margarine
Parsley
1 lb tomatoes or tomato purée, optional

Well grease a round baking-tin, and arrange the sprats in a circle, with their tails to the middle. Sprinkle them with plenty of salt, and pepper and lemon juice, and repeat the layers until the dish is full, covering the top with tiny bits of butter or margarine, with minced parsley. Bake until the sprats are done [about forty minutes in a moderate oven, Mark 4 or 350°F (180°C)], and serve in the same dish. Tomatoes in slices or in purée can be added to the layers, if wished, and, I am inclined to think, with advantage.

WHITEBAIT

[The whitebait should be rolled in seasoned flour and deep fried.] Odd as it may sound, cold fried whitebait make a really excellent luncheon if they are served with a salad. They should be sprinkled with lemon juice.

CRAB AUX OEUFS

White meat of a cooked crab
1 oz butter
½ teacup milk
Salt and pepper
6 eggs
½ teaspoon chopped parsley
Pinch cayenne pepper
Mushrooms, optional
A little extra butter, some cream or an egg is optional

A delicious light dish. Flake up the white meat of a cooked crab.
Melt an ounce of butter in a stewpan or casserole and add salt,
pepper and half a teacupful of milk. Put in the crab meat and warm
it through. Lightly beat half a dozen eggs, add them to the
mixture, and stir on a slow heat till they thicken. Then add half a
teaspoonful of chopped parsley and a pinch of cayenne pepper, and
serve immediately, remembering that the eggs go on cooking in
the pan after it has come off the fire. A spoonful or two of cream
or a little butter [or an extra egg] may be stirred in, off the fire, at
the last, and will prevent any chance of it going leathery. You
might, as a matter of fact, add a few chopped mushrooms to this
dish with advantage, putting them in when the crab meat is
introduced, but you would then want to use just a little less milk
to compensate for the moisture from the mushrooms.

CRAB FRIED IN BATTER

Crab flesh makes a good fritter, and what could be easier than this?
Chop up the crab meat coarsely, season it with salt and pepper, dip
spoonfuls of it in fritter batter and fry in deep fat. It is odd, but
excellent, to serve a light mustard sauce [see page 125] with these,
using French not English mustard in the making.

MUSSELS À LA CATALANE

[Make sure that the mussels are cleaned well as described on page 19 as the cooking liquor is used as part of the dish. Also discard any dead mussels, i.e. those that remain open before they are cooked, or any that remain closed after they are cooked.]

    2 quarts mussels
    1 onion
    Parsley stalks
    Flour
    Butter or margarine
    Squeeze lemon juice
    Black pepper

Open the mussels quite simply by putting them into a saucepan without any water, sprinkling them with a little salt, covering them with a wet cloth, and letting them steam until the shells begin to open [see page 19] but have in the pan also a little minced onion, parsley stalks, and coarsely ground pepper. When they are done, take off one shell from each and keep the mussels hot, while you strain the liquor from the mussels and let it reduce a little. Now make a sauce by frying some chopped onion in butter or margarine, sprinkle with flour and moisten with the mussel liquor to which you have added a squeeze of lemon juice. Pour this over the mussels after straining again.

MUSSELS, FRIED

    2 quarts mussels
    Butter or margarine
    1 chopped onion
    1 clove garlic
    Parsley
    Breadcrumbs

Clean and 'open' the mussels as in previous recipe. Then take them out from the shells, and fry them in a frying-pan with butter or good margarine, some chopped shallot or onion, garlic and parsley chopped together and some breadcrumbs. Shake the pan well while they are frying, and when the breadcrumbs are golden, serve at once.

FISH PANCAKE

Any cooked fish may be used to make a pancake, and very good it is. Flake or chop it up, mix it with an ordinary pancake batter, and cook it as one large and rather thick pancake, or several small ones.

Suitable fish to use can be found among the following: smoked haddock, kipper, salmon, lobster, crab, prawns, shrimps. Where suitable, a variation can be got by flavouring the batter slightly with cheese or mixed herbs. The pancake should be cooked first on one side, then turned over with a spatula and finished on the other side with a little more fat in the pan. It should be served flat, as if it is rolled or folded it will probably break.

FISH PIE WITH PASTRY

[Any white fish can be used for this recipe, cod, smoked haddock, whiting, and to make it stretch extra hard-boiled eggs could be added. I would recommend making one turnover for two people rather than one large one for four as the end bits are always nice. Flaky pastry is used in this pie and very good results can be had with frozen or packet pastry as flaky pastry is rather laborious to make for a simple supper dish.]

> 1 lb cooked white fish
> ½ pt white sauce made with milk and the water the fish
>   was cooked in
> Chopped parsley
> 2 hard-boiled eggs
> ¾ lb flaky pastry

Flake up some cooked fish, and mix it with chopped parsley and hard-boiled chopped egg, binding it with white sauce made with milk and fish stock. Roll some flaky pastry to a square of the size you want, put the fish mixture, when cold, in the middle, and fold the corners of the pastry to the middle, after damping the edges. Pinch the edges firmly together, and bake in a hottish oven [Mark 5 or 375°F (190°C)] for half an hour. Various additions according to your taste and pocket may be made to the contents of this pleasant turnover, and the sauce might be flavoured with cheese if preferred.

SARDINES—A TIP!

In the good old days you always used to find a bayleaf included in the best sardines. Nowadays it is worth while opening your tin of sardines some hours before you want it, turning them into a receptacle with a bayleaf underneath them, and leaving them thus, well covered, until you want them. You will be surprised that even in that short time the flavour will have permeated them. It would be better still to crumble some bayleaves over them as well, but only the very enthusiastic can be expected to pick these bits off before the sardines are served.

Vegetables including Salads

Beetroot, Fried · Broad Beans and Bacon · Broad Bean Purée with Peas · Broccoli, Italian Fashion · Brussels Sprouts and Bacon · Celeriac with Mustard · Courgettes Niçoises · Gratin de Courgettes · Roasted Artichokes · Red Cabbage · Leek Hash · Sham Whitebait (Marrow) · Grilled Mushrooms à la Bourguignonne · Mushrooms à la Bordelaise · Mushrooms à la Tunisienne · Ragoût of Onions · Peas and Beans · Potato Pancakes · Potato Soufflé · Potatoes with Chives · Fried Pumpkin Cakes · Spinach Patties · Watercress Purée · Potato and Bacon Salad · Potato Salad · Nasturtium Leaf Salad · Beetroot and Dandelion Salad · Salad Delilah · ·Watercress Salad · Haricot Bean and Sorrel Salad · Broccoli Salad

VEGETABLES

BEETROOT, FRIED

1 cooked beetroot
1 beaten egg
1 tablespoon flour
1 tablespoon white wine
Salt, pepper, pinch of nutmeg
Breadcrumbs mixed with chopped parsley

Beetroot is usually a one-fashion dish, boiled hot or boiled cold, the first cut in cubes and served with melted butter, or white sauce, and chopped parsley, the second dressed as a salad. But beetroot like almost everything else can be fried. Cut a cooked beetroot into long slices. Dip these into a batter made of a mixture of beaten egg, a tablespoonful of white wine, a tablespoonful of flour, salt, pepper and a trifle of nutmeg. Then roll the slices in fine breadcrumbs mixed with chopped parsley, and fry them. Drain them well and serve at once.

BROAD BEANS AND BACON

Shelled young broad beans
Fattish bacon
Chopped parsley or savory
Parsley
Butter or margarine

A simple country dish of beans and bacon is made as follows. Put a layer of fat bacon cut in dice in a casserole or stewpan, and then add a layer of shelled broad beans, seasoning with a little pepper, chopped parsley or savory, and a few flakes of butter or margarine. Repeat these layers until the casserole is full, leaving the top one of bacon. Then put the lid on tightly, and bake in a slow oven [Mark 3 or 325°F (170°C)] for an hour. Uncover and eat with pleasure and gratitude.

BROAD BEAN PURÉE WITH PEAS

    1 lb shelled young broad beans
    1 sliced Jerusalem artichoke
    Handful of shelled green peas
    3 lettuce leaves
    1 small onion
    Salt, pepper, pinch of sugar
    Butter or margarine
    Cream if available

This is so good that it may well form a course by itself. Measure out a pound of broad beans after they have been shelled (they should be young ones), and boil them with a sliced Jerusalem artichoke, a handful of shelled green peas, a few lettuce leaves and a small onion. When the vegetables are done, put them through a sieve [or blended]. Put the purée back into the pan and stir it over a low heat until it begins to thicken, then add a few small pieces of butter or margarine, and a seasoning of salt, pepper and just a touch of sugar. If you can manage a couple of spoonfuls of cream at the very end, so much the better; but in any case whisk it up well, pile it in a dish, and serve surrounded by fingers of cheese-flavoured pastry [see page 115].

BROCCOLI, ITALIAN FASHION

    1 broccoli, or cauliflower
    Breadcrumbs
    Few capers
    6 stoned black olives
    1 anchovy fillet
    Butter

Cut the broccoli, or cauliflower, into flowerets, and cook them carefully. Put them into a dish, and sprinkle over them some fine breadcrumbs mixed with a few capers, stoned olives and an anchovy fillet, all chopped up very small. Pour plenty of melted butter over this and put the dish in the oven for ten minutes to brown, and then serve it.

BRUSSELS SPROUTS AND BACON

1 lb Brussels sprouts
6 oz bacon
Grated cheese

Cook and drain some Brussels sprouts, the smaller and tighter the better. Dice six ounces of bacon and fry until crisp. Take out the bacon dice, and fry the sprouts in the fat for about five minutes, tossing them now and again. Add the bacon dice and cook all together for a minute or so, turning out on to the serving-dish and sprinkling with grated cheese.

CELERIAC WITH MUSTARD

1 celeriac
2 oz butter or margarine
1 teaspoon French mustard

Cook the celeriac in strips for about half an hour, and when done, pour off the liquid and let the strips dry a little. Meanwhile, cream some butter or margarine with a little mustard, French mustard being best. Put this mustard butter or margarine into the pan with the celeriac, let it melt very slightly and then toss the strips in it. Serve at once.

COURGETTES NIÇOISES

[Courgettes (zucchini in U.S.A.) are well known to us now and are widely available.]

    1 lb courgettes
    1 lb skinned tomatoes
    Butter
    Salt and pepper
    Chopped tarragon

The most delicious vegetable marrow are the tiny ones, not more than four inches long, which can be cooked whole or cut in quarters. Stew some tomatoes in butter (they should be skinned and have their pips removed) until they are a purée, season this well, and stew the little peeled marrows in it. When done sprinkle with a little chopped [French] tarragon and serve either hot or cold.

GRATIN DE COURGETTES

[This is a good vegetarian main course with baked potatoes to accompany it perhaps.]

    1 lb courgettes
    2–3 tablespoons thin cream
    Grated cheese
    1 beaten egg
    Butter or margarine
    Salt and pepper

Take some baby marrows [courgettes], scrape them lightly, chop them up finely and put them into a wide saucepan with just enough water to prevent them from catching, about a tablespoonful. Add a pinch of salt, and stir and cook them until the moisture has evaporated. Then add a little butter or good margarine, some thin cream, grated cheese to taste and a beaten egg. Mix, pepper lightly, and pour into a shallow fireproof dish. Sprinkle liberally with grated cheese, dot with butter or margarine, and brown quickly in a hot oven.

ROASTED ARTICHOKES

A very unusual way of serving this vegetable is to peel the Jerusalem artichokes, and cook them under the meat in exactly the same way as roast potatoes. They will get rather discoloured, but this will not matter, as their flavour will make up for their looks!

RED CABBAGE

½ large or 1 small red cabbage
1 oz butter or margarine
1 eating apple
1 teaspoon finely chopped onion
Salt, cayenne pepper, grated nutmeg
1 dessertspoon brown sugar
Pinch of powdered cloves and cinnamon
1 tablespoon vinegar
Cooked chestnuts, optional

Red cabbage makes a delicious hot dish, which is not as well known as it should be. Slice the cabbage finely and leave it to soak in cold water for half an hour. Then put it into a stewpan in handfuls straight out of the water without draining it, and add an ounce of butter or margarine, a peeled cored and sliced eating apple, a teaspoon of very finely chopped onion, a saltspoon of salt, a touch of cayenne pepper and a little grated nutmeg. Do not add any more liquid, but put on the lid and cook gently for an hour, stirring now and then to bring the cooked cabbage to the top.

At the end of the hour, add a dessertspoon of brown sugar (or failing that ordinary sugar, or even honey would do), a pinch of powdered cloves and cinnamon and a tablespoon of good vinegar. Cook for another five minutes or so and serve very hot. This is particularly good with boiled knuckle of pork. White cabbage can be cooked in the same way. Extra substance can be added in the form of pieces of cooked chestnuts.

LEEK HASH

 1 lb leeks
 Butter or margarine
 Good pinch of flour
 Salt, pepper and grated nutmeg
 1 cup of milk or cream
 1 beaten egg
 Sippets of fried bread for garnish

A poor translation of the name of a famous French dish, *Poireaux en Hachis*, which everyone should try once, and will have often again. Cook the white part of the leeks, keeping the edible parts of the green leaves for a soup, and cook them until tender in salted water. Then drain them as well as possible and chop them up finely. Put a good bit of butter or margarine in a saucepan, and when it has melted add the chopped leeks with a good pinch of flour, and a seasoning of salt, pepper and grated nutmeg. Mix well together and cook a little without browning the flour at all, then moisten with a cupful of milk. (In time of plenty, this should be cream, and then it is a dish for the gods!) Cook a little longer for the sauce to thicken and then bind with an egg. Garnish with sippets of fried bread.

SHAM WHITEBAIT

 Vegetable marrow
 Flour
 Frying fat
 Cayenne pepper
 Quarters of lemon
 Brown bread and butter

This is not a fish, but a rather amusing way of cooking an elderly marrow which is even beyond the stuffing stage. Parboil it, then cut up part of it into little strips about the size of whitebait. Roll them in a floured cloth, and fry them quickly in boiling fat. When they are golden, drain them and serve them dusted with cayenne pepper, garnished with quarters of lemon and brown bread and butter handed with them.

GRILLED MUSHROOMS À LA BOURGUIGNONNE

[Ambrose Heath recommends old brandy for this recipe; a modest brandy would suffice.]

> Mushrooms
> Clove of garlic
> Finely chopped shallot to taste
> Parsley
> Butter
> Liqueurglass old brandy
> Salt and pepper

Snail addicts will welcome this dish, since the butter used in it is the same as that with which *Escargots Bourguignonne* are stuffed. Grill the mushrooms in the usual way, and when they are done surmount each with a pat of this exquisite if a little expensive butter. Pound a clove of garlic to a paste, adding finely chopped shallot, minced parsley, salt and pepper freshly ground from the peppermill. Mix this with the butter, adding a liqueurglassful of old brandy. If you do not like garlic, this dish is not for you.

MUSHROOMS À LA BORDELAISE

> Mushrooms, large ones
> Olive oil
> 2 shallots to 1 lb mushrooms
> Bunch parsley
> Lemon juice
> Salt
> Freshly ground black pepper

So many of us ask especially for small mushrooms when we buy them that this excellent way of cooking large ones may be welcomed. Choose the thickest and firmest, and score the underside of each across in lozenges. Leave them to marinate, gill side downwards, for two hours in olive oil seasoned with salt and pepper, and then grill them. Now mince two or three shallots, and fry them in oil or butter with half their bulk of minced parsley, adding salt, pepper and a good squeeze of lemon juice. As soon as the shallot has begun to colour properly pour this mixture over the mushrooms which you will have arranged top downwards in the dish. In the seasoning of this dish it is best to use freshly ground black pepper.

MUSHROOMS À LA TUNISIENNE

½ lb mushrooms
2 tablespoons olive oil
1½ tablespoons tomato purée
Squeeze lemon juice
Bouquet of parsley, thyme and bayleaf
Salt
Freshly ground black pepper

Mushrooms make a much favoured hors d'oeuvre and this is a well-flavoured way of making one. Get some mushrooms and cut them in quarters, they should be smallish ones. Put into a shallow saucepan two tablespoonfuls of olive oil and one and a half tablespoonfuls of concentrated tomato purée, a little lemon juice, a bouquet of parsley, thyme and a bayleaf, salt and some freshly ground black pepper. When this is pretty hot, add the mushrooms and cook on a goodish heat with the lid on for ten minutes or so, shaking the pan now and then. Then take out the bouquet at once, turn the mushrooms and their sauce into a serving dish, and leave until quite cold.

RAGOÛT OF ONIONS

2 lb small onions [shallots if available]
2 oz butter
2 tablespoons white wine
4 cloves
Small stick of cinnamon
2 bayleaves
½ pt stock
½ lb tomatoes

This excellent hot ragoût comes from Smyrna. Fry two pounds of small onions in two ounces of butter till golden brown. Then add two tablespoonfuls of white wine, a few cloves, a small stick of cinnamon and two bayleaves. Add also half a pint of good stock and half a pound of tomatoes rubbed through a sieve. Simmer for about an hour, or until the onions are tender, and serve very hot.

PEAS AND BEANS

Green peas
French or runner beans
Butter or margarine
Parsley and chervil

For this charming dish you want some young French or runner beans. Cook them, and some green peas separately, and when the beans are done cut them into small pieces about the same size as the peas. Then put the two vegetables together in a pan with a bit of butter or margarine, shake them together, adding a chopping of parsley and chervil, and serve them as hot as possible. An unusual and fascinating combination.

POTATO PANCAKES

¾ lb potatoes
Good ¼ pt milk
1 tablespoon butter or margarine
Salt
1½ eggs
Grated cheese

Boil three-quarters of a pound of potatoes, rub them through a
sieve or potato masher, and mix them with just over a quarter of a
pint of milk, a tablespoonful of butter or margarine, a little salt
and an egg and a half. Beat into a light batter, and cook like
ordinary pancakes, serving them sprinkled with grated cheese.

POTATO SOUFFLÉ

1 pt potato purée, made with about 1½ lb potatoes
A little double cream
3 eggs
Salt and pepper

For potato soufflé you want about a pint of potato purée enriched
with a little cream, well-whipped and fairly stiff. To this add the
yolks of three eggs and their whites stiffly whisked. Season it well
and cook in a buttered soufflé-dish for about a quarter of an hour
in a moderate oven [Mark 4 or 350°F (180°C)].

POTATOES WITH CHIVES

[Simple but delicious!]

Potatoes
Sour cream
Chives
Butter
Salt and pepper

It is easy enough to mix some chopped chives with your mashed potatoes, as you can to your mayonnaise, but this recipe gives the real touch. Mash the potatoes in the usual way with butter and a little more pepper than usual. Then, instead of moistening them with milk, use some sour cream, and then whip in your chopped chives as well. If you have the sour cream but no chives, then very young green of spring onions will do as a good substitute.

FRIED PUMPKIN CAKES

[To cook the pumpkin, you can either steam it, covered, over a pan of boiling water until it is tender, or bake it in the oven after you have cut it into smallish pieces and removed the seeds and stringy bits.]

    2 breakfastcups cooked pumpkin
    Salt and pepper
    1 teaspoon sugar
    1 teaspoon tomato ketchup
    ½ teacup milk
    5 dessertspoons melted margarine or butter
    Salt, and pepper
    3–4 bacon rashers

Mash up two breakfastcupfuls of cooked pumpkin, and mix in half a level teaspoon of salt, a dash of pepper, a level teaspoon of sugar, a teaspoon of ketchup, half a teacup of milk and three dessertspoons of melted margarine.

Mash all together well, and shape into flat round cakes. Fry the rashers of bacon and pour off all the fat but three dessertspoons. Fry the pumpkin cakes golden on each side in this, and serve with the bacon rashers.

D

SPINACH PATTIES

Hot spinach purée
4 oz flour
2½ oz melted butter or margarine
1 beaten egg
1¼ oz grated cheese
Salt, pinch sugar
A little milk

Put four ounces of flour into a bowl, and mix in two and a half ounces of melted butter or margarine, a saltspoon of salt, one whole beaten egg, a pinch of sugar and an ounce of grated cheese. Make a pliant paste with a spoonful of milk or so. Roll out and line some patty tins with this paste [prick them with a fork], and bake them empty. Then fill them with a hot purée of spinach, sprinkle a little grated cheese on top, and brown them quickly.

WATERCRESS PURÉE

1½ lb watercress
1 oz butter or margarine
1 dessertspoon flour
3–4 tablespoons stock or milk
Salt and pepper

This is cooked in the same way as the French cook spinach, and it is called *Cresson en Epinards*. For four or five people you will want about a pound and a half of watercress, which you must pick over carefully and wash well before using. Then cook it in plenty of rapidly boiling water, salted, without the lid on the pan. Boil hard for a quarter of an hour, then turn into a colander and plunge this at once into cold water. Drain the cress as well as you can, pressing it between the hands, and then put it on a board and chop it finely.

Put it now into a pan with two 'walnuts' of butter or margarine, and stir on a quick fire for five minutes, until all the steam has evaporated. Then season with salt and pepper, sprinkle with a dessertspoonful of flour, mix well, cook for a minute or two, and then add three good tablespoonfuls of stock or milk. Stir until it boils, then cover and simmer very gently for twenty minutes or so. Stir in a few bits of fresh butter or margarine on serving this very delicious dish.

SALADS

POTATO AND BACON SALAD

Cut up into small pieces some potatoes boiled in their skins, and do it while they are still hot. Mix with a few rashers of streaky bacon crisply fried and cut in small pieces, adding the fat which came from the frying. Mix in a warm salad bowl, adding a little vinegar and sprinkling with chopped parsley and, if possible, chopped chives or the green part of spring onions. [Eat this salad while it is still warm.]

POTATO SALAD

This is a French family recipe. The salad can be eaten hot or cold, but it must be seasoned when still hot. Cook the potatoes, which should be small waxy ones, peel them and cut them in rings. Then pour over them a dressing made by mixing together (for every pound and a half of potatoes) four tablespoonfuls of olive oil, one of vinegar, two of red or white wine, three or four of cold stock, a coffeespoonful of salt, a pinch of pepper, chopped parsley, chervil, tarragon and chives, and if you like a little mustard.

NASTURTIUM LEAF SALAD

[This is worth making just for its looks! The scarlet flowers are so pretty. Use the French dressing on page 130.]
These leaves are rather hot for some, but they make quite a good salad if dressed with salad dressing, and decorated, if you feel like it, with a flower or two from the plant.

BEETROOT AND DANDELION SALAD

[The dandelions must be very young ones for this salad. See note on growing, page 16.]
Dandelion may sometimes be bought in shops, but usually it grows for nothing, and all you have to do to make them ready for eating is to blanch them by putting over the plants a flat stone or a tile, or a flower pot. If you do come by any, use the hearts only, and mix them with about the same quantity of cooked beetroot. Dress with French dressing of olive oil, vinegar, salt and pepper.

SALAD DELILAH

Was it this that tempted Samson? Chop up fairly finely some bananas and apples, and mix them with thin julienne strips of celery. Dress with mayonnaise.

WATERCRESS SALAD

A Swedish fashion. Mix the watercress with slices of peeled and cored apple. After dressing with salad dressing, sprinkle with a little chopped fennel and marjoram. [I would use a French dressing here as on page 130.]

HARICOT BEAN AND SORREL SALAD

[The haricot beans need to be soaked overnight if possible and then cooked until tender. Use the French dressing on page 130.]
I have found that a haricot bean salad, plainly cooked and not tinned ones, mixed with thin strips of raw sorrel makes a very good mixture, the slight acidity of the sorrel contrasting very pleasantly with the starchiness of the cold beans. Salad dressing, of course.

BROCCOLI SALAD

The broccoli used for this salad should be very young. Soak the broccoli in cold salted water for about half an hour, break it into flowerets, tie these loosely in a piece of muslin, and cook them in boiling salted water for about ten minutes. They should still be rather firm when cooked. Drain them and let them get quite cold. (The muslin is simply to make it easier to remove them from the water.) Make a dressing of tarragon vinegar, salt, pepper, a little sugar, and four tablespoonfuls of olive oil. Mix well with a fork and add, if you like, a teaspoonful of tomato ketchup. Put the broccoli flowerets in a salad bowl, and add a few chopped anchovy fillets. Dress with the mixture, turning the broccoli over carefully so as not to break the heads.

Puddings

Apple Charlotte · Apple Suzanne · Apples in Wine · Bonde Pige med Slør · Banana Toad in the Hole · Banana Soufflé · Cashew Nut Soufflé · Cherry Pudding · Chestnuts and Prunes · Baked Figs · Fig Flan · Gooseberry Pudding, Baked · Grapefruit Cream · Guava Fool · Honey Custard · Marmalade Cream · Marmalade Tart · Pears in Cheese Pastry · Baked Quinces · Rhubarb Pie · Rhubarb Butterscotch Pie · L'Ami des Enfants · Toffee Pudding · Bread and Butter Pudding · Chocolate Pancakes · Pancakes with Nuts · Christmas Omelette · Frozen Plum Pudding

APPLE CHARLOTTE

4–5 slices thin bread and butter
Golden syrup
Apple purée made with 2 lb apples
Approximately 2 cups fine fresh white breadcrumbs
Cream, optional

Line the charlotte mould with thin slices of bread and butter (no crusts), and spread them as thickly as you can with golden syrup. Meanwhile, you have made a purée of stewed apples, not too thin, and this you will now put into the mould in alternate layers with fine breadcrumbs. Let the breadcrumbs be the last layer, and cook this lovely pudding in the oven [Mark 4 or 350°F (180°C)] till it is brown, about thirty to forty minutes, as it will be not only on the top but on the sides, too. It only wants some thick cream, or Devonshire cream, to make it one of the world's superlative sweets.

APPLE SUZANNE

Butter
2 lb apples
2 oz brown sugar
$\frac{1}{2}$ grated lemon rind
1 tablespoon apricot jam
Icing sugar
Cream, optional

Melt some butter in the bottom of a pan and stew in it some peeled and quartered apples, with brown sugar, grated lemon rind and apricot jam. Stir well so as to prevent it from burning, and when it is done put it into a small fireproof dish, sprinkle the top copiously with icing sugar, and put it into a moderate oven [Mark 4 or 350°F (180°C)] until the sugar begins to caramelize and form a crust. Then serve hot with cream.

APPLES IN WINE

[Use sweet dessert apples, such as Cox's Orange Pippins, and be careful not to over-fill the dish.]

2 lb cored apples, or more depending on size of dish
Castor sugar
1 glass red wine
Whipped cream

Peel and cut some apples in thin slices and lay them in a deep buttered dish, sprinkling each layer liberally with castor sugar. Fill the dish right up to the brim and then pour over a large glass of red wine. Put on the lid or a plate and press it well down. Cook in a slow oven [Mark 2 or 300°F (150°C)] for four hours. The apples will by then have become a deep red jelly, which can be turned out and served in a glass or other dish covered with whipped cream.

BONDE PIGE MED SLØR

A famous Scandinavian sweet which, being translated, means Peasant Girl with a Veil.

3 cups stale brown breadcrumbs
Butter
Sugar
A thick apple purée made with 2 lb apples
Raspberry jam
Whipped cream

Crumble some stale brown breadcrumbs, spread them on a baking-tin, and bake them in the oven with a little butter and sugar sprinkled over them. Stir them now and again to keep the crumbs separate, and to keep your eye on them as they may burn quickly and suddenly. While they are still hot, spread a layer of them in a dish, cover this with thick apple purée and this again with raspberry jam. Repeat these layers until the dish is nearly full, and when quite cold, cover the top with plenty of whipped cream.

BANANA TOAD IN THE HOLE

3 large bananas
1 tablespoon sugar
4 oz flour
1 pt water
1 tablespoon salad oil
2 eggs, separated

Rather queer-sounding, but good all the same. Make a batter with four ounces of flour, a pint of water, a tablespoonful of salad oil and two eggs, folding in the whisked whites last of all. Put half this batter into a greased fireproof dish, then put in three good-sized bananas cut in rings, sprinkle these with sugar, and cover them with the rest of the batter. Bake in a quick oven, until set and browned [Mark 6 or 400°F (200°C) for about 25 minutes].

BANANA SOUFFLÉ

4 large bananas
1 tablespoon flour
1 tablespoon castor sugar
1 breakfastcup hot milk
Yolks of 2 eggs
Whites of 3 eggs
A nut of butter
Icing sugar

Cut four large bananas in half lengthwise, keeping the skins intact. Mash the flesh through a fine sieve. Now mix a level tablespoonful of flour and the same of castor sugar in a breakfastcupful of hot milk. Bring to the boil and cook a little longer, stirring well. When it is thick, add the yolks of two eggs, a small piece of butter, the stiffly whipped whites of three eggs, and the mashed bananas. Fill the banana skins with this mixture, and bake for about eight minutes in a hot oven [Mark 6 or 400°F (200°C)]. A little icing sugar can be sprinkled over each just before they are ready.

CASHEW NUT SOUFFLÉ

6 sponge fingers
6 macaroons
½ pt hot milk
3 eggs, separated
1 teacup sugar
1 level teaspoon salt
1 teaspoon vanilla essence
1 breakfastcup cashew nuts, peeled and chopped
Whipped cream

This is as attractive as it is unusual. Take half a dozen sponge fingers and the same number of macaroons, and soak them in half a pint of hot milk. Arrange them in the bottom and round the sides of a buttered baking-dish, and pour in any milk left over. Now beat well three yolks of eggs with a teacupful of sugar, a level teaspoonful of salt, and a teaspoonful of vanilla essence. Add a breakfastcupful of chopped and peeled cashew nuts, and fold in the three stiffly-whisked egg whites. Pour this mixture into the baking-dish, and bake in a moderate oven [Mark 4 or 350°F (180°C)], for half an hour or until it is firm and well browned on top. Serve at once, handing whipped cream.

CHERRY PUDDING

1½ lb [stoned] black cherries or 1 large tin
3 tablespoons flour
3 eggs

Pinch salt
1½ pt milk
3 tablespoons castor sugar

Put three tablespoonfuls of flour and a pinch of salt into a bowl and break and mix into it, one by one, three eggs. Add a pint and a half of milk by degrees, and three tablespoonfuls of castor sugar. Put about a pound and a half of black cherries into a fireproof dish, and pour this mixture over them. Bake it in the oven [Mark 4 or 350°F (180°C), until it is set] and serve it with more sugar sprinkled on the top. It will take about half an hour.

CHESTNUTS AND PRUNES

Chestnuts [see page 24 for method of cooking]
Prunes
Sugar
Powdered cinnamon to taste
Lemon juice
A little sherry

Cook some chestnuts and separately some prunes. Drain the prunes and mix them with the chestnuts, flavouring them with a little sugar, powdered cinnamon and lemon juice. Pour over them some of the liquor in which the prunes were cooked, flavoured with sherry, serve hot.

BAKED FIGS

There is nothing to compare with a fig fresh and ripe from the tree, but the small imported ones may be treated in this way.

Wash them well and leave the skins on. Put them into a fireproof dish with sugar and very little water, and bake them slowly, pricking them with a fork and basting them now and again with the syrup. Serve them in the same dish when they are cold, with vanilla or rum-flavoured cream.

FIG FLAN

6 oz shortcrust pastry, made with 4 oz flour to 2 oz fat
½ lb dried figs, soaked overnight
2 eggs, separated
2 tablespoons castor sugar plus a little extra for meringue
1 teaspoon lemon juice

Line a flan case with pastry, and bake it with a rice or haricot bean filling in a hot oven for a quarter of an hour. Soak half a pound of dried figs overnight, and after draining them, cut them in little pieces and stew them in half a pint of boiling water until they are soft. Beat the yolks of two eggs with two tablespoonfuls of castor sugar, add this to the figs and their water, and stir and cook until it begins to thicken. Then add a teaspoonful of lemon juice, and spread the mixture into the flan case. Now beat the two egg whites with a little sugar until stiff, decorate the top of the flan with this meringue, and bake for six or seven minutes [Mark 7 or 425°F (220°C)] until the meringue is lightly browned.

GOOSEBERRY PUDDING, BAKED

[If you have an electric blender use it instead of sieving the gooseberries. I would cook this pudding in a moderate oven, Mark 4 or 350°F (180°C).]

6 oz shortcrust pastry, made with 4 oz flour to 2 oz fat
1 quart gooseberries
½ oz butter or margarine
1 egg
¼ pt breadcrumbs
Sugar

Stew a quart of topped-and-tailed green gooseberries in as little water as possible until they are tender, then sieve them, and add to them half an ounce of butter or margarine, a beaten egg, a quarter of a pint of breadcrumbs, and sugar to taste. Line a pie-dish with shortcrust pastry, and after filling it with the gooseberry mixture, bake the pudding for about forty minutes.

GRAPEFRUIT CREAM

1 orange
2 grapefruit
Lump sugar
1 pt thick cream
Stale sponge cake

Rub some lump sugar over an orange and a grapefruit so that it grates off the outside of the rinds. Then pound it up as finely as you can. Squeeze out the juice of these two fruits and add the juice of another grapefruit. Then mix the whole well with a pint of thick cream. Lay some slices of stale sponge cake on the bottom of the dish in which it will be served, and pour the cream over it. Let it stand all the afternoon in a very cold place, and serve as cold as you possibly can.

[This was written in pre-refrigerator days!]

GUAVA FOOL

[The pancake Mousseline biscuits which Ambrose Heath recommends are not available any more but a good biscuit would be a Dutch fan wafer.]

1 tin guavas
Cream [double cream is called for here, whipped a little]

The slightly acid taste of the guavas makes this sweet quite distinctive. Buy a tin of guavas, and pass the contents through a hair sieve [or blend]. Whip it well, adding as much syrup from the tin and cream as you think desirable. Get your grocer to order you some

Pancake Mousseline Biscuits, made by Le Gal of London, for you
to eat with it.

HONEY CUSTARD

    1 pt milk
    2 eggs
    Pinch salt
    1 teacup honey
    Powdered cinnamon

Scald a pint of milk. Mix together two slightly beaten eggs, a good
pinch of salt, and a teacupful of honey: add the milk slowly,
stirring until the honey is dissolved. Bake [in a tin of hot water in
a moderate oven Mark 4 or 350°F (180°C) until set], and when
cold sprinkle with powdered cinnamon.

MARMALADE CREAM

[One or two beaten egg whites can be added to make this lighter.]

    1 dessertspoon marmalade
    1 tablespoon brandy
    Juice ½ lemon
    Castor sugar
    Pint of cream

Chop up finely a dessertspoonful of orange marmalade, add a
tablespoonful of brandy, the juice of half a lemon, and as much
castor sugar as you like. Mix all this with a pint of cream, and
whip it well until it is thick. Pile into a dish and serve.

MARMALADE TART

    6 oz shortcrust pastry, made with 4 oz flour to 2 oz fat
    About ½ jar of marmalade
    2 egg yolks
    2 egg whites

Make an open tart, and fill it with marmalade which you have mixed with the yolks of two eggs and the whites whipped very stiffly. Bake in a moderate oven [Mark 4 or 350°F (180°C)] until done. [You can tell when the tart is done by very lightly touching the surface to see if it is set. It takes about half an hour.]

PEARS IN CHEESE PASTRY

½ lb cheese-flavoured shortcrust pastry using:
    8 oz flour
    4 oz butter or margarine
    2 oz grated cheese
    Pinch salt

Cooked or tinned pears
Brown sugar
Butter

Seekers after the exotic may like to try this example. Make some cheese-flavoured pastry (but not too much cheese), roll out an eighth of an inch thick, and cut into four-inch sided squares. Put half a well-drained, cooked or tinned pear on each pastry half, and fill the hollow where the core has been with a teaspoonful of brown sugar and half a teaspoonful of butter. Fold over the other half of the pastry to make a triangle, press the edges together with a fork, and prick a few holes in the top. Bake in a hot oven for about a quarter of an hour [Mark 6 or 400°F (200°C)]. Serve hot. Apples could be treated in the same way.

BAKED QUINCES

2 lb quinces
Sugar
Macaroon crumbs, optional

Quinces are so seldom eaten by themselves in this country, save in the form of a jam or a jelly, that this recipe may be welcome to those who like their perfumed flavour.

See that they are ripe, wash them, peel them, cut them in half and core them, and lay them, cored side upwards, in a greased [flameproof] baking-dish. Boil the peel and cores in enough water to cover them for twenty minutes, then strain off the liquid. Now put a level of teaspoonful and a half of sugar in each quince half, pour over two tablespoonfuls of the quince liquid, and bake covered in a slow oven [Mark 2 or 300°F (150°C)] for about three hours, or until the quinces are quite soft. They will turn a rich deep red colour. You can then either serve them as they are, or sprinkle them over with plenty of macaroon crumbs, add a few shavings of butter, and brown quickly in a hot oven.

RHUBARB PIE

[This is one of the few rhubarb recipes that I have found which does not need lashings of extra sugar on it when it is being served to make it taste less tart. Very good. The next recipe is delicious, too.]

> ½ lb shortcrust pastry
> 1½ breakfastcups of ½-inch pieces of rhubarb, about 2 lb
> 1 teacup sugar
> 3 level dessertspoons flour
> 1 egg
> Squeeze lemon or orange juice, optional

Cut some young rhubarb into half-inch long pieces, and measure out a breakfastcupful and a half of them. Mix together a teacupful of sugar and three level dessertspoonfuls of flour, and bind this with an egg. Add this to the rhubarb, and use it to fill a pastry-lined pie-plate or shallow fireproof dish. Cover with a top crust and bake [in a moderate oven Mark 4 or 350°F (180°C) for about thirty-five minutes]. A touch of lemon or orange juice may be added to the rhubarb if liked, and it may be noted here that if the rhubarb is first scalded and then left to get cold before being used, some of its acidity will be lost and less sugar will be needed.

RHUBARB BUTTERSCOTCH PIE

4–6 oz shortcrust pastry
3 breakfastcups of chopped uncooked rhubarb
¾ teacup brown sugar
2 level dessertspoons flour
Pinch salt
2 beaten eggs

Line a pie-plate with pastry and fill it with three breakfastcupfuls of chopped uncooked rhubarb. Mix together the brown sugar, two level dessertspoonfuls of flour and a dash of salt, and two beaten eggs, and spread this over the rhubarb. Bake in a hot oven [Mark 6 or 400°F (200°C)] for ten minutes, then reduce the heat to moderate [Mark 4 or 350°F (180°C)] and bake for another twenty to twenty-five minutes, when the rhubarb should be tender and the custard set. Young pink rhubarb of course is best.

L'AMI DES ENFANTS

12 sponge cakes
1½–2 lb fresh fruit
Brown sugar
1 breakfastcup milk

A good old-fashioned sweet that we used to enjoy in our far-away childhood. Butter a mould or a pie-dish and line it with split sponge cakes, using the undersides only. Now fill up the dish with layers of fresh fruit and brown sugar, and add a breakfastcupful of milk, for a dozen sponge cakes. Now dip the top half of the sponge cakes for a second only in water, and cover the top of the pudding with them. Bake in a moderate oven [Mark 4 or 350°F (180°C)] for half an hour and serve hot.

E

TOFFEE PUDDING

½ lb demerara sugar
½ lb golden syrup
¼ lb butter or margarine
¾ lb stale bread
Milk

We are all particularly fond of this. Boil together in a large frying-pan half a pound of demerara sugar, half a pound of golden syrup and a quarter of a pound of butter or margarine until they are golden brown. Cut three-quarters of a pound of stale bread (no crusts) into squares about half an inch thick, and soak them well in milk. Drain them on a tray, and when the liquid toffee is ready, put the squares of bread into it, and let them get as hot as possible without burning. Then serve them piled up high in a dish, and may I, without indecency, suggest clotted cream?

BREAD AND BUTTER PUDDING

A luncheon long ago at the Orleans Club with E. V. Lucas, at which the high spots were a magnum of Krug and a cold bread-and-butter pudding, converted me once and for all to a sweet which in childhood had always been regarded with suspicion and some distaste. On my return from St. James's, I immediately set out to discover a recipe for this pudding for myself, and found this one, which I have never found surpassed.

About 6–8 thin slices of bread and butter, using stale bread
A handful each of currants and sultanas
Mixed spice
1 pt milk
4 oz sugar
Vanilla pod of essence
4 egg yolks and 1 whole egg

Cut some thin slices of stale bread and remove the crusts. Butter the slices, and sprinkle over them some currants and sultanas which have first been swelled in tepid water and then well drained. Put these slices into a pie-dish, sprinkle them with a little spice, and cover them with the following custard: boil a pint of milk with four ounces of sugar. Then either infuse it with a vanilla pod for twenty minutes (this is best), or flavour it with vanilla essence. Whisk up four egg yolks and one whole egg in a basin, and pour the milk by degrees over them, whisking as you do so. Now pour the whole thing through a fine sieve into another basin, leave it for a few minutes, and then carefully remove every vestige of froth from the surface. Pour this over the bread and butter slices, and cook in a moderate oven [Mark 4 or 350°F (180°C)] in a tin of hot water, until the custard is set. It definitely should be eaten when quite cold. [I would not be quite so definite, personally I enjoy this pudding warm, or even hot.]

CHOCOLATE PANCAKES

[I would recommend unsweetened chocolate, especially if this pudding is for adults.]

2 oz flour
2 tablespoons milk
4 egg yolks
2 egg whites
1 tablespoon castor sugar
Pinch salt
2 tablespoons cream
Grated chocolate

Make a batter with two ounces of flour, two tablespoonfuls of milk, the yolks of four eggs and the whites of two, beaten separately, a tablespoonful of castor sugar, and a pinch of salt. Beat well with two tablespoonfuls of cream, and then fry some very

small pancakes, browning them on one side only. Sprinkle the
unbrowned side with grated chocolate so as to cover the surface
completely, roll the pancakes up, sprinkle them with a little sugar,
and lay them in a greased tin. Bake for twenty minutes in a
moderate oven [Mark 3 or 325°F (170°C)] and serve at once.

PANCAKES WITH NUTS

[To make the batter, sieve the flour and the salt into a bowl, break
the egg yolks into a well in the middle and stir the flour in slowly.
Add the milk and beat well. Add the sugar and the lemon rind
and finally fold in the stiffly whisked egg whites. Leave to stand
for as long as possible.]

> 4 oz flour
> Pinch salt
> 1 tablespoon castor sugar
> Grated rind lemon
> 2 eggs, separated
> ½ pt milk
> Walnuts
> Pistachio nuts
> Double cream

Make a batter and [after leaving it to stand] fry the pancakes.
    Fill the pancakes with a mixture of pounded walnuts and pista-
chio nuts and warm thick cream.

CHRISTMAS OMELETTE

> 6 eggs
> 1 tablespoon sugar
> Pinch salt
> 2 tablespoons cream
> Pinch grated orange or lemon rind
> 1 tablespoon rum plus some warm rum
> Hot mincemeat

Beat up six eggs with some sugar and a pinch of salt, and add two tablespoonfuls of cream, a pinch of grated orange or lemon rind and one tablespoonful of rum. Cook the omelette in the usual way, and before folding it, stuff it with plenty of hot mincemeat. Put it on a long dish, sprinkle it with warm rum, and set it alight at table.

FROZEN PLUM PUDDING

This might be suitable for Christmas Day in the Antipodes!

$\frac{1}{2}$ teacup each currants and seedless raisins
$\frac{1}{2}$ teacup candied peel
2 tablespoons shredded dates
2 tablespoons shredded figs
12 maraschino cherries
1 teacup sugar syrup flavoured with maraschino
2 tablespoons chopped blanched almonds
1 quart chocolate ice cream

Simmer half a teacupful of washed and picked currants and the same quantity of seedless raisins in a very little water for five minutes, or until they are plump, then drain them and let them get cold. Shred half a teacupful of candied peel, and shred enough dates to make two tablespoonfuls, and the same of figs. Chop up a dozen maraschino cherries and put these with the figs, dates and candied peel into a teacupful of syrup strongly flavoured with maraschino, and leave them there for six hours. Mix them now with the currants and raisins and two tablespoonfuls of chopped blanched almonds, amalgamate all with a quart of chocolate ice cream, and freeze in the refrigerator for two to four hours.

Sauces

Barbecue Sauce · Caper Sauce (Italian) · Chilli Sauce · Cream Sauce for Game · Fennel Sauce · Greek Fish Sauce · Mustard Sauce · Orange Sauce for Wild Duck or Game · Peanut Butter Sauce · Prune Sauce · Sauce aux Noix · Tomato Sauce · Chervil Sauce · Fluffy Cucumber Sauce · Cumberland Sauce · Horse-radish Sauce · Vinaigrette Sauce · Apricot Sauce · Caramel Sauce · Chocolate Sauce · Coffee Sauce · Honey Cream Sauce · Marmalade Sauce · Marshmallow Sauce · Melba Sauce · Mince-meat Sauce · New Forest Sauce · Orange Sauce

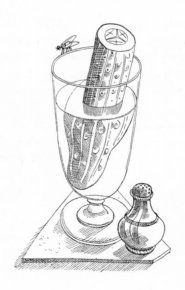

SAVOURY SAUCES

BARBECUE SAUCE

6 teaspoons melted butter, about 1 oz
1 dessertspoon vinegar
½ teacup red currant jelly
¼ level teaspoon dry mustard
Salt, cayenne pepper

Mix together all the ingredients adding salt and cayenne pepper to taste. Use for heating up slices of cold lamb and mutton.

CAPER SAUCE (ITALIAN)

[Very good with mutton or boiled cod.]

1 minced anchovy
4 oz capers
3 tablespoons vinegar
Chopped parsley
Oil and butter

Mince an anchovy and let it melt in a little oil and butter over a gentle heat. Add four ounces of capers, three tablespoonfuls of vinegar and some chopped parsley. Serve hot or cold.

CHILLI SAUCE

[This sauce would be good to 'pep' up boiled white fish or meat.]

1½ breakfastcups vinegar
6 tomatoes
4 green peppers
1 onion
1 scant tablespoon sugar

Boil a breakfastcupful and a half of vinegar, and add to it six chopped tomatoes, four chopped green sweet peppers, a minced onion and a scant tablespoonful of sugar. Boil all together for an hour, then strain, season to taste, and serve with any fish or meat.

CREAM SAUCE FOR GAME

Thicken the drained drippings in the pan from roasting game with flour, let it brown a little, and then moisten with cream, fresh or sour. When thick and smooth, season with salt and pepper. If sour cream is used, add a touch of lemon juice at the last.

FENNEL SAUCE

9–10 sprigs fennel
5 tablespoons olive oil
2 tablespoons tomato purée [fresh purée is best but if
    tomatoes are not available use tinned]
Salt and pepper
Pinch flour
Grated nutmeg

In France a savoury fennel sauce is made as follows: Blanch, dry and chop very finely the leaves from nine or ten sprigs of fennel. Then heat slowly in a small pan on a slow fire four tablespoonfuls of olive oil, and when it begins to get hot, add a tablespoonful of fresh tomato purée and half the fennel with salt and pepper. Mix it all well together and sprinkle in a good pinch of flour. When this is coloured, add, stirring all the time, another spoonful of oil and another of tomato purée, the rest of the fennel and a hint of grated nutmeg. Mix well again, and let it simmer slowly uncovered for ten minutes, stirring it now and again. Butter can be used instead of oil, but this will rob the sauce of the true Provençal flavour.
[Especially good with boiled salmon or mackerel.]

GREEK FISH SAUCE

1 tablespoon flour
2–3 cloves garlic
½ glass vinegar
1 glass hot water
1 leaf of rosemary
Salt and pepper

Mix in a tablespoonful of flour with the fat left in the pan after frying fish, adding two or three crushed cloves of garlic, salt, pepper, half a glass of vinegar, a glassful of hot water and a leaf of rosemary. Stir and boil until thick, and then strain.

MUSTARD SAUCE

1 tablespoon melted butter
1 tablespoon white wine
Mustard to taste

Whip well over a gentle heat a tablespoonful of melted butter, the same of white wine and mustard to taste. Do not allow to boil.

ORANGE SAUCE FOR WILD DUCK OR GAME

2 oranges
1 oz butter
1 oz flour
½ pt stock or gravy
Salt and pepper

Make an infusion from the thinly peeled rind of two oranges, and let it soak for ten minutes. Now make a sauce with an ounce of butter, an ounce of flour and half a pint of stock or gravy, and cook for a quarter of an hour or so, letting it reduce a little. Add a tablespoonful of the infusion from the orange rinds and the juice

of the two oranges, season with salt and pepper, and heat through
to serve.

PEANUT BUTTER SAUCE

[This would be interesting with boiled ham or roast chicken.]

    3 dessertspoons butter
    3 dessertspoons peanut butter
    3 tablespoons flour
    ¾ pt chicken stock
    Salt and pepper

Brown lightly three dessertspoonfuls of butter, add the same
quantity of peanut butter and when well mixed, stir in three
tablespoonfuls of flour. Let this brown, and then add gradually
three-quarters of a pint of chicken stock. Stir while this thickens,
then season with salt and pepper, and serve.

PRUNE SAUCE

    1 lb small prunes
    2 lemons
    4 blades mace
    2 dozen whole cloves
    Bunch allspice
    1 peppercorn
    2 cups sugar
    ½ cup cider vinegar

Certainly there is no better relish for game, mutton, lamb, fowls
of every sort, even roast pork, provided it be tender and crisp
enough. Wash a pound of small prunes and put them in plenty of
cold water with the juice of two lemons and their thin yellow peel,
four blades of mace, two dozen whole cloves, and a bunch of
whole allspice, reinforced with a single peppercorn. Cook for two
hours, simmering gently and filling up as the water wastes. Then

put in two cups of sugar and simmer another hour until the syrup is thick and rich. Then add half a cup of cider vinegar, let it boil five minutes, and your sauce is done.

SAUCE AUX NOIX

Handful of walnuts
Oil
1 clove garlic or less
Little parsley
Boiling water, about 1 tablespoon
A little olive oil

An unusual sauce to serve with spaghetti. Peel a handful of walnuts and pound them well in a mortar. Fry in oil a very small quantity of garlic and a little parsley, finely chopped together; add the walnut purée, cook a little but do not brown. Moisten with a little olive oil and very little boiling water. Mix well with the hot spaghetti and serve immediately.

TOMATO SAUCE

¼ onion
½ stick celery
Few leaves of basil
Bunch parsley
½ cup olive oil [or corn oil]
8–9 tomatoes, sliced
Salt and pepper

Mince finely a quarter of an onion, half a stick of celery, a few leaves of basil and a bunch of parsley. Add half a cupful of olive oil, a pinch of salt and pepper, and eight or nine ripe tomatoes cut in slices. Boil all together until the sauce is thick and creamy, and then strain through a sieve and serve. [Simmer this sauce, rather than boil; it will take at least half an hour.]

CHERVIL SAUCE

Double cream
Fresh chervil
Salt and pepper

Season some fresh double cream with salt and pepper, and mix in
finely cut fresh chervil. Serve with [hot or cold] roast chicken.

FLUFFY CUCUMBER SAUCE

1 medium cucumber
1 carton double cream, 5 oz size, fresh or sour
3 teaspoons [white wine] vinegar [or lemon juice]
Salt

Peel, chop and drain well a medium-sized cucumber. Whip
stiffly a teacupful of double cream, fresh or sour, and fold in the
cucumber with a little salt and three teaspoonfuls of vinegar.
Serve with cold fish or meat.

CUMBERLAND SAUCE

4 tablespoons red currant jelly
1 glass port
1 shallot
1 teaspoon orange rind
1 teaspoon lemon rind
1 teaspoon mustard
Juice of 1 orange
Juice of ½ lemon
Cayenne pepper
Pinch powdered ginger

An admirable cold sauce can be made as follows. Dissolve four
tablespoonfuls of red currant jelly, and add a good glass of port, a

teaspoonful of finely chopped and blanched shallots, the same of orange rind cut in julienne strips and blanched, the same of lemon rind similarly treated, a teaspoonful of mustard, a little cayenne pepper and powdered ginger, the juice of an orange and the juice of half a lemon. Mix all well together. It is particularly good with cold venison, and with cold mutton, too.

HORSERADISH SAUCE

2 tablespoons finely grated horseradish
¼ pt thick cream
½ teaspoon made mustard
½ teaspoon castor sugar
½ teaspoon tarragon vinegar

Mix together, in this order, half a teaspoonful of made mustard, the same of castor sugar, the same of tarragon vinegar, two table-spoonfuls of finely grated horseradish and a quarter of a pint of slightly whipped cream. The cream should be mixed in lightly, and the sauce stood on ice until it is wanted. It is recommended for chicken or game and for hot and cold salmon [also beef].

VINAIGRETTE SAUCE

1 teacup French dressing [see below]
1 teaspoon chopped green peppers
1 teaspoon chopped chives
1 teaspoon parsley
1 teaspoon capers
1 tablespoon pickled cucumber

To a teacupful of ordinary French dressing add, in this order, a tablespoonful of chopped green peppers, a teaspoonful each of chopped chives, parsley and capers, and a tablespoonful of chopped pickled cucumber. Stir well together before serving with beef or lamb.

[FRENCH DRESSING—*Editor's recipe*

　1–2 tablespoons vinegar, preferably wine vinegar
　4–6 tablespoons oil, corn, vegetable or pure olive
　Pinch dry mustard
　Pinch of castor sugar
　Salt and pepper—black pepper freshly milled

Put the salt, pepper, mustard and sugar into a screw top jar, add
the vinegar and shake until it is well mixed. Add the oil and shake
well before tasting to check the seasoning.]

SWEET SAUCES

[Any of these sweet sauces would be delicious with sponge
puddings, ice cream, meringues or even pancakes.]

APRICOT SAUCE

　2 tablespoons apricot jam
　2 oz sugar
　1 glass white wine

Mix together two tablespoonfuls of apricot jam, two ounces of
sugar and a glass of white wine, and warm for five minutes over
the fire.

CARAMEL SAUCE

[Especially good with ice cream.]

　1 breakfastcup sugar
　1 cup coffee
　$\frac{3}{4}$ cup water

Put a breakfastcupful of sugar in a thick metal saucepan, and melt it over a moderate heat, stirring all the while, until it is a light brown. Then add slowly a quarter of a cupful of clear coffee and three-quarters of a cupful of water, and boil for six minutes.

CHOCOLATE SAUCE

[It is worth using the best quality plain chocolate for this sauce.] The best and really only chocolate sauce is made simply by dissolving chocolate with a very little water, sweetening and flavouring it as desired, and then by finishing it with cream and butter in small pieces. Nothing can possibly compare with this smooth richness.

Note   A discreet touch of cinnamon is nearly always an improvement to chocolate sauces, as is the addition of a little strong black coffee, which seems to enhance the flavour of the chocolate. In the same way, the addition of a very little chocolate to a coffee sauce seems to bring out the flavour of the coffee.

COFFEE SAUCE

2 tablespoons strong black coffee
2 eggs yolk
1 tablespoon castor sugar

Whip in a basin over boiling water, two tablespoonfuls of very strong black coffee, two yolks of eggs and a tablespoonful of castor sugar. When creamy-thick it is ready.

HONEY CREAM SAUCE

⅓ breakfastcup cream
¼ cup honey
1 teaspoon lemon juice

Whip a third of a breakfastcupful of cream until thick, then add a quarter of a cup of honey and a teaspoonful of lemon juice. Whip all the time until well mixed.

MARMALADE SAUCE

1 breakfastcup marmalade
2 wineglasses white wine

Put a breakfastcupful of orange marmalade into a saucepan with
two wineglassfuls of white wine. Stir over a gentle heat until very
hot, then strain.

MARSHMALLOW SAUCE

[Children would enjoy making this, and eating it too!]

4 oz marshmallows
1 breakfastcup icing sugar
¼ cup boiling water

Cut four ounces of marshmallows into pieces with a pair of scissors,
and melt them in a double saucepan. Dissolve a breakfastcupful of
icing sugar in a quarter of a cup of boiling water, add this to the
marshmallows, and stir until well mixed.

MELBA SAUCE

[The classic sauce to accompany vanilla ice cream and peaches,
but good with other fruit also.]

1 breakfastcup sieved raspberries and juice
1 teacup red currant jelly
1 teacup sugar
1½ level teaspoons cornflour or arrowroot
3 teaspoons cold water

Mix together a breakfastcupful of sieved raspberries with their
juice, a teacupful of red currant jelly and the same of sugar. Bring
to the boil, and when the jelly is quite melted, thicken with a level
teaspoonful and a half of arrowroot or cornflour mixed smoothly
with three teaspoonfuls of cold water. Strain again, and cool.

MINCEMEAT SAUCE

[Try it with ice cream or a plain sponge pudding. Delicious and quick!]

     1 teacup water
     1 teacup sugar
     1 breakfastcup mincemeat

Boil a teacupful of water with the same quantity of sugar for five minutes, and then add a breakfastcupful of mincemeat.

NEW FOREST SAUCE

     $\frac{1}{4}$ lb butter
     $\frac{1}{4}$ lb castor sugar
     1 tablespoon brandy
     2 tablespoons sherry
     Pinch nutmeg

Beat up a quarter of a pound of fresh butter and a quarter of a pound of castor sugar until white and light, beating them over a pan of hot water. Add a tablespoonful of brandy and two of sherry, with a very little nutmeg. Add the sherry and brandy by slow degrees, and beat all together until thoroughly mixed. Serve in a sauce-boat, particularly with Christmas pudding.

ORANGE SAUCE

A mixture of two-thirds orange marmalade and a third apricot purée or jam. Flavour with curaçao.

A Sweet and Savoury Miscellany

*Frosted Fruit · Peanut Nougat · Orange Jumbles · Hot Choco-
late · Elderflower Champagne · Cherry Jam · Elderflower and
Rhubarb Jam · Quince and Orange Marmalade · Quince Honey ·
White Strawberry Jam · Parsley Jelly · Jam Chutney · Chilli
Vinegar · Italian Mustard · Pickled Eggs · Minted Cream Cheese ·
Anchovy Butter · Horseradish Butter · Shrimp Butter · Tarragon
Butter · Tunny Fish Butter*

FROSTED FRUIT

Strawberries, raspberries, cherries, and red or white currants respond very readily to this simple treatment. First beat up the white of an egg in half as much water. (You can do this easily by measuring the egg white in a glass.) Then dip your fruit in this, seeing that it is well covered, and now drain it for a moment, and roll it in castor sugar until it is well coated. Shake it so that any extra bits of sugar drop off, and spread the coated fruit out on a large sheet of white kitchen paper to dry. It will take three or four hours in a warm or sunny room, and looks very grand when finished.

PEANUT NOUGAT

Shell and roast some peanuts, and measure out a breakfastcupful of them, chopped. Melt a pound of granulated sugar in a heavy pan, stirring continuously until it is a thin syrup. Then add the nuts and a pinch of salt, and stir until the nuts are well coated. Spread them thinly in an ungreased tin, and mark into squares when nearly cold.

ORANGE JUMBLES

A useful and delicious biscuit which can be served with cream or fruit.

> ¼ lb almonds shredded
> ¼ lb white sugar
> 3 oz butter
> 2 oz flour
> Grated juice and rind of 2 oranges
> Drop of cochineal

Shred the almonds and mix them with the sugar, butter, flour and the grated rind and juice of two oranges. Mix this well together and colour with a drop or so of cochineal. Drop this mixture by teaspoonfuls on a greased baking-tin, and bake in a fairly slow oven till the biscuits are done. They should be set pretty widely apart in the tin, as each will spread out to about the size of a teacup rim. To say that they are indescribably charming really describes them.

[They will take about 15–20 minutes at Mark 3 or 325°F (170°C), but keep an eye on them.]

HOT CHOCOLATE

Chocolate is prepared in the same way as cocoa. Choco or, as the Americans call it, Mexican Chocolate, may be appreciated by some. This is a mixture of three parts made chocolate and one part very strong black coffee. The coffee is added after the chocolate is made, and whipped cream is handed with it. A little rich for breakfast, perhaps!

ELDERFLOWER CHAMPAGNE

    2 large heads elderflower, in full bloom
    1 gallon cold water
    1 lemon
    2 tablespoons white vinegar
    1½ lb lump sugar

Squeeze the juice from the lemon, and cut the rind into four pieces. Put this with the flowers, sugar, and vinegar into a large jar or pan, pour on the water and leave for twenty-four hours. Strain, and bottle in screw-stoppered bottles, and keep for several weeks before using.

CHERRY JAM

    4 lb stalked black cherries
    3 lb sugar [preserving sugar is best]
    1 tablespoon lemon juice
    2 tablespoons orange juice

Put a layer of sugar in the bottom of the preserving-pan and then a layer of cherries. Repeat these layers and then add the lemon and orange juice. Put the pan over a very low heat, and when the sugar begins to melt, keep on shaking the pan so that it does not burn. As soon as the sugar is all dissolved, boil fairly quickly, still shaking and not stirring so that the cherries remain whole. When the syrup sets, the jam is done, and excellent it is.

ELDERFLOWER AND RHUBARB JAM

6 lb rhubarb
2 handfuls of opened elderflowers
6 lb sugar [preserving sugar is best]
2 lemons

This is well-worth making, for it has an elusive taste of Muscat grapes about it. Peel and cut six pounds of rhubarb in pieces, and put it into a large bowl. Put two handfuls of fully opened elderflowers, picked in the sun, in a muslin bag and press it down into the middle of the rhubarb so that it is covered, then sprinkle six pounds of sugar over it. Cover, and leave for twelve hours, then stir it, cover again, and leave for another twelve hours. Now put it all into a preserving-pan, heat it up but do not boil, then put it back into the bowl for another twenty-four hours. Now take out the elderflowers, and add the grated rind and juice of two lemons, and boil up in the preserving-pan until the jam will set.

QUINCE AND ORANGE MARMALADE

3½ lb quinces
4 oranges
4½ lb sugar [preserving sugar is best]
3 pt water

Wash, peel and core the quinces, and put the skins and cores into a saucepan with the water. Boil them until tender and then strain the juice through muslin. Put this juice into a preserving-pan with the quinces finely chopped and the rind of two of the oranges also finely chopped, and cook slowly until the quinces are tender. Then add the warmed sugar and the strained juice of all four oranges, stir till the sugar is dissolved, and boil all together until the marmalade sets.

QUINCE HONEY

    5 large quinces
    5 lb sugar [preserving sugar is best]
    1 pt boiling water

Peel and grate the quinces. Heat the water and sugar to dissolve it, add the quinces and cook for a quarter of an hour to twenty minutes. It should look like honey when cold.

WHITE STRAWBERRY JAM

    4 oz strawberry jam
    4 oz red currant jelly
    2 egg whites

Here's something for children to make for their own tea; but they must make it themselves, for the joy of seeing a red jam turn white. First whisk together two egg whites until the white will stand up on the whisk, then mix these with four ounces of strawberry jam and four ounces of red currant jelly, and go on whisking until, unbelievably, the mixture becomes white. Perhaps cousins or friends to tea, and a relay of little arms to do the whisking, is the best time for this experiment.

PARSLEY JELLY

    Parsley
    1 lemon, or more
    Lump sugar

An old-fashioned preserve that used to be served with cold chicken and other meats. Fill a saucepan with parsley leaves, and barely cover them with cold water. Bring to the boil and simmer gently for half an hour. Then measure the liquid and add the juice of a large lemon and its rind for every pint. Strain, measure again, and allow a pound of lump sugar to each pint of the liquid. Boil until the jelly sets, and pot in small jars, covering them when cold.

JAM CHUTNEY

If a chutney is wanted in a hurry, this simple recipe can be used. Put any jam such as black currant, plum or damson, into a bowl and mix with it vinegar, salt, red pepper, sultanas, blanched, sliced and pounded almonds and a little garlic if liked. Stir well together, and bottle.

CHILLI VINEGAR

[This chilli vinegar will add spice to salad dressings and curries.] Cut some small dried chillies in halves, and quarter-fill your bottles with them. Bring some cider or white wine vinegar to the boil, and when it has cooled, fill the bottles up. Cork closely and store.

ITALIAN MUSTARD

Put into a small saucepan a tumbler of white wine, a small onion stuck with six cloves and a little salt. Simmer over a very low fire for a quarter of an hour, then strain through a sieve, and stir in by degrees four ounces of mustard powder. When smooth and thick, pot in jars.

PICKLED EGGS

[I like pickled eggs with salads or as a snack with drinks.]

    16 hard-boiled eggs
    ½ oz each black peppercorns, whole ginger and allspice
    1 quart vinegar

Put the shelled eggs into wide-mouthed jars; boil the spices with the vinegar for ten minutes, and pour it boiling over the eggs. Cover closely when cold.

MINTED CREAM CHEESE

Beat up some cream cheese with a little cream, salt and very finely minced fresh mint leaves, allowing about a tablespoonful of mint to three ounces of cheese.

SAVOURY BUTTERS

Savoury butters play an important part in the preparation of many savouries and are invaluable for making canapés, as well as many garnishes.

ANCHOVY BUTTER

Take the fillets from a dozen anchovies, and pound them with a quarter of a pound of butter, passing the mixture afterwards through a fine sieve.

HORSERADISH BUTTER

Grate a couple of ounces of horseradish and pound with a quarter of a pound of butter. Put through a fine sieve.

SHRIMP BUTTER

Pound cooked shrimps or shrimp trimmings with an equal quantity of butter, add a touch of lemon juice. Sieve.

TARRAGON BUTTER

Blanch and pound some tarragon leaves, and use them to flavour your butter as you like it.

TUNNY FISH BUTTER

Pound up a tin of tunny fish [tuna], and mix it with your butter, seasoning it with a little lemon juice. Pass through a sieve.

Index